Lizzie McGuire

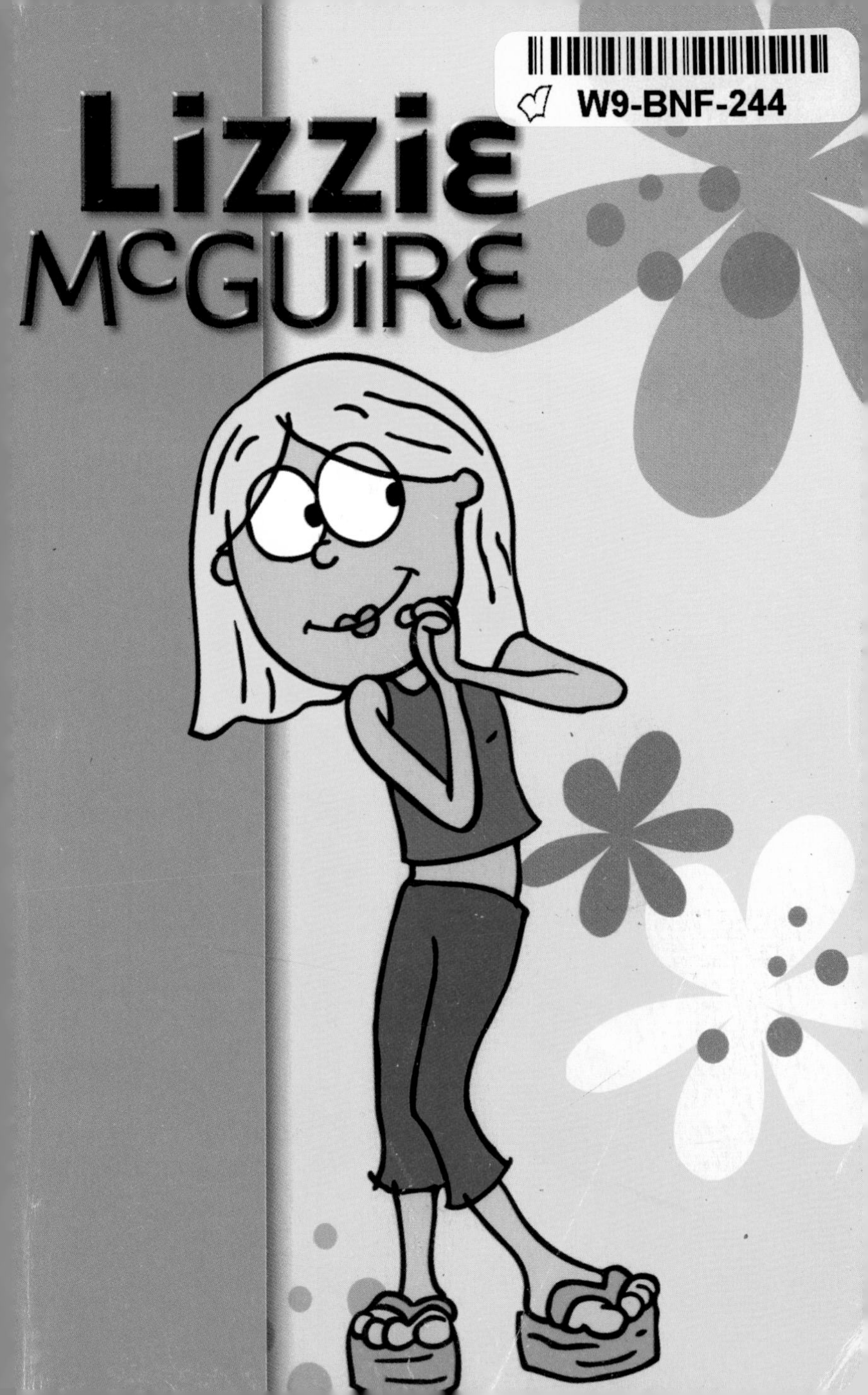

ALSO AVAILABLE FROM TOKYOPOP®

MANGA

*INDICATES 100% AUTHENTIC MANGA (RIGHT-TO-LEFT FORMAT)

CINE-MANGA™

NOVELS

TOKYOPOP KIDS

ART BOOKS

ANIME GUIDES

062703

For more information visit www.TOKYOPOP.com

Lizzie McGuire

Volume 2

Series created by Terri Minsky

"Rumors"
written by Melissa Gould

"Jack of All Trades"
written by Trish Baker

LOS ANGELES • TOKYO • LONDON

Graphic Design & Lettering - Yolanda Petriz
Production Specialist - Anna Kernbaum
Cover Layout - Patrick Hook

Senior Editor - Amy Court Kaemon
Managing Editor - Jill Freshney
Production Coordinator - Antonio DePietro
Production Manager - Jennifer Miller
Art Director - Matt Alford
Editorial Director - Jeremy Ross
VP of Production - Ron Klamert
President & C.O.O. - John Parker
Publisher & C.E.O. - Stuart Levy

Email: editor@TOKYOPOP.com
Come visit us online at www.TOKYOPOP.com

A **TOKYOPOP**® Cine-Manga™
5900 Wilshire Blvd., Suite 2000, Los Angeles, CA 90036

ISBN: 1-59182-148-7

First TOKYOPOP printing: July 2003

10 9 8 7 6 5 4 3 2 1
Printed in Canada

LIZZIE McGUIRE

Volume 2

CONTENTS

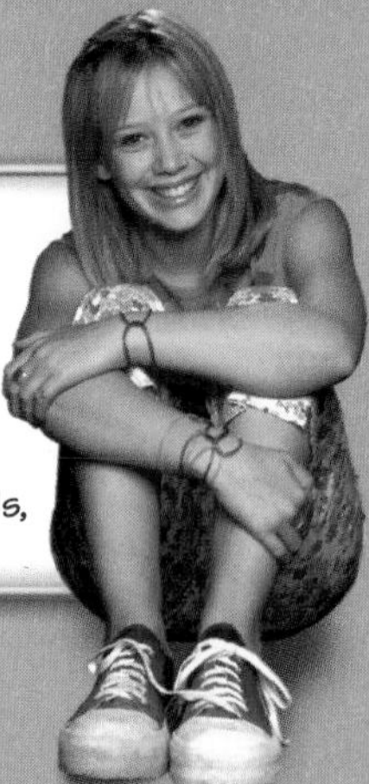

LIZZIE MCGUIRE
A typical 14-year-old girl who has her fair share of bad hair days and embarrassing moments. Luckily, Lizzie knows how to admit when she's wrong, back up her friends, and stand up for herself.

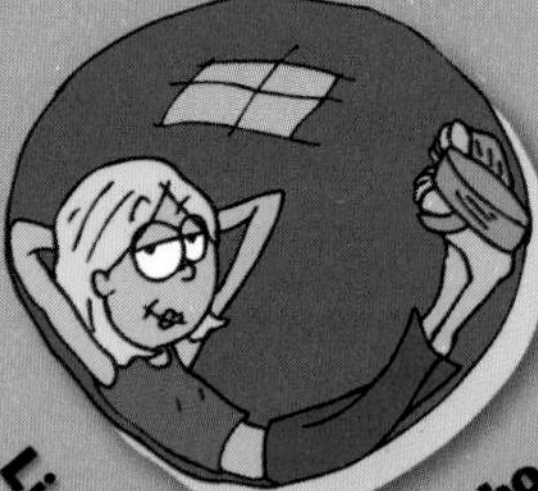

Lizzie's alter-ego, who says and does all the things Lizzie's afraid to.

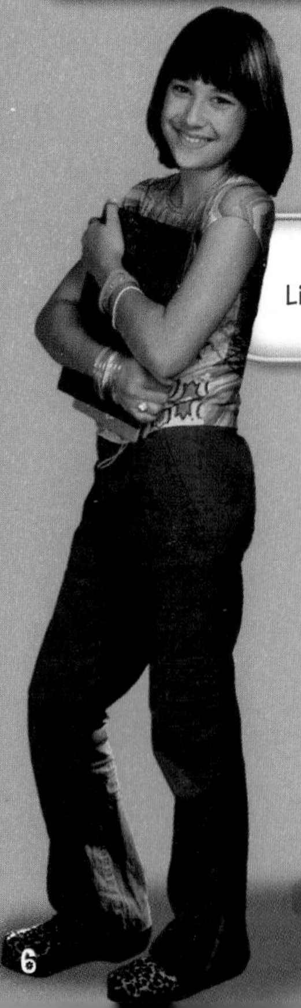

MIRANDA
Lizzie's best friend.

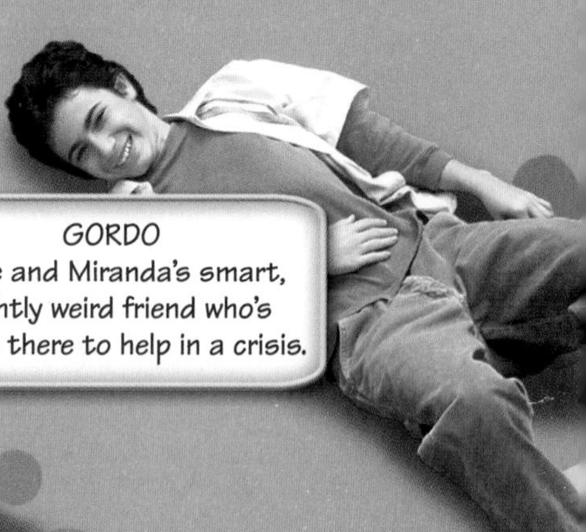

GORDO
Lizzie and Miranda's smart, slightly weird friend who's always there to help in a crisis.

KATE
Lizzie and Miranda's now popular ex-friend, who seems to be good at everything she does.

DANNY
The cutest guy at school.

MR. PETTUS
Lizzie's science teacher.

MATT
Lizzie's little brother, who spends most of his time making her crazy.

LIZZIE'S MOM,
She only wants the best for Lizzie, but sometimes she tries a little too hard.

LIZZIE'S DAD
He loves Lizzie, though he doesn't always know how to relate to her.

Lizzie McGuire

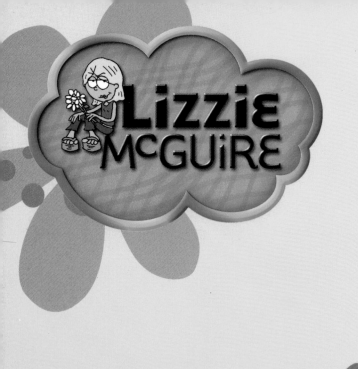

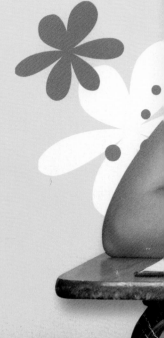

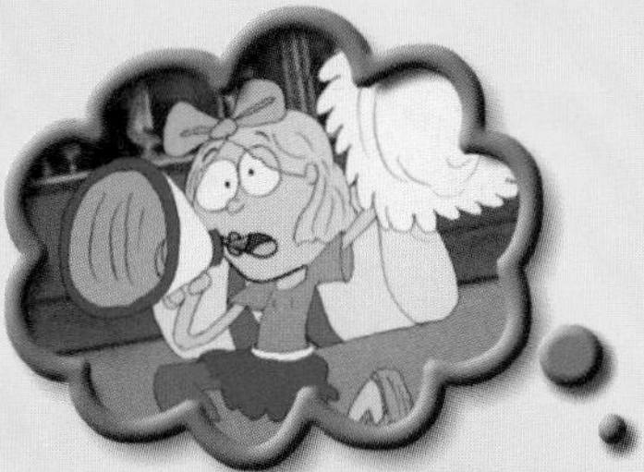

Episode 3

"Rumors"

Lizzie decides to try out for cheerleading, but ends up accidentally starting a juicy rumor about one of the girls on the squad. When Miranda stands up to take the blame, Lizzie learns what being a true friend is all about.

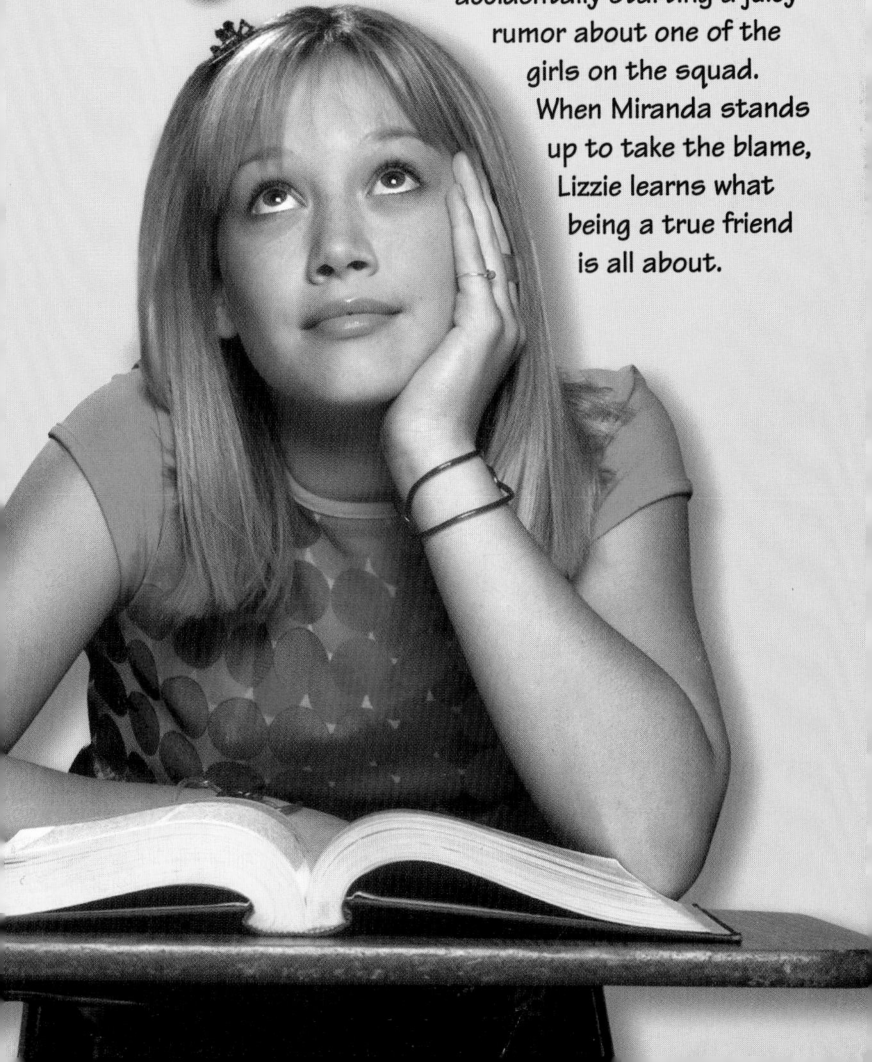

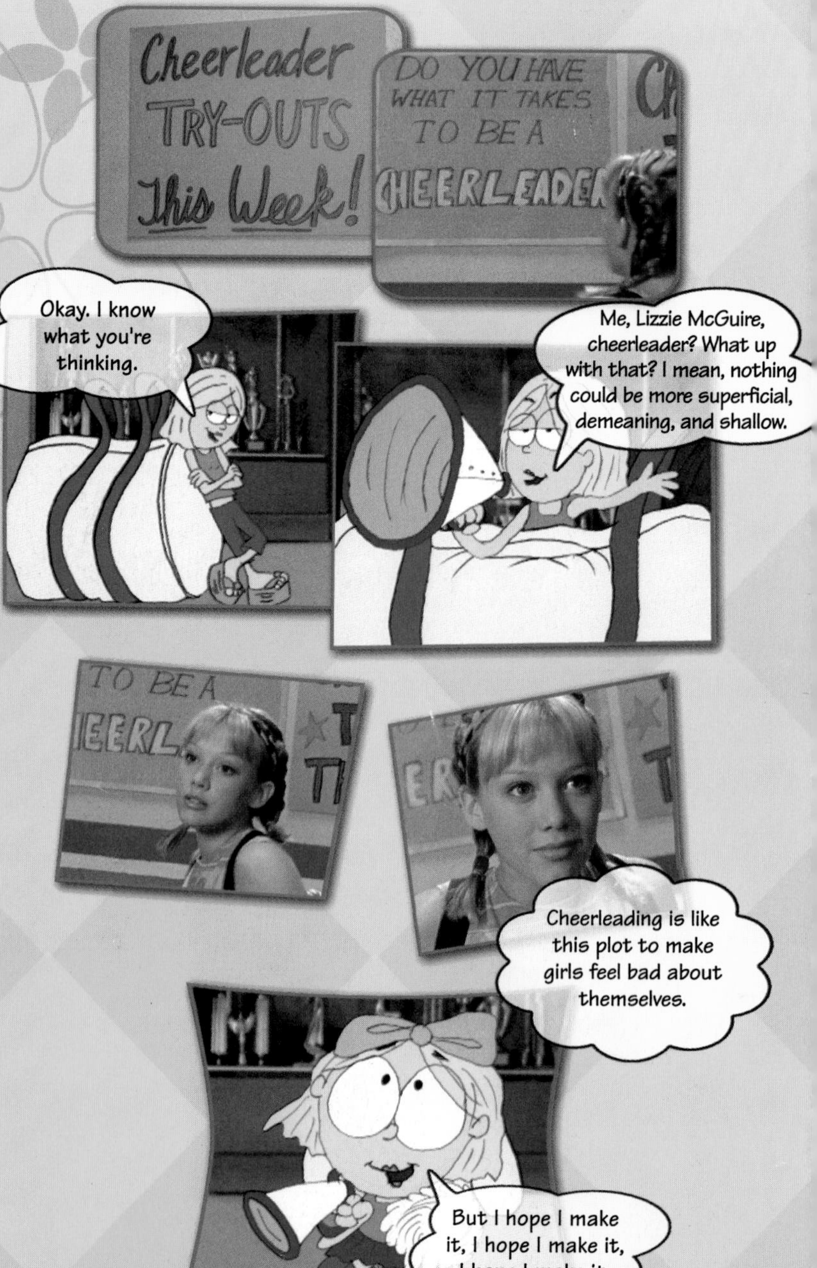
Cheerleader TRY-OUTS This Week!
DO YOU HAVE WHAT IT TAKES TO BE A CHEERLEADER
Okay. I know what you're thinking.
Me, Lizzie McGuire, cheerleader? What up with that? I mean, nothing could be more superficial, demeaning, and shallow.
Cheerleading is like this plot to make girls feel bad about themselves.
But I hope I make it, I hope I make it, I hope I make it.

LATER, IN THE CAFETERIA...

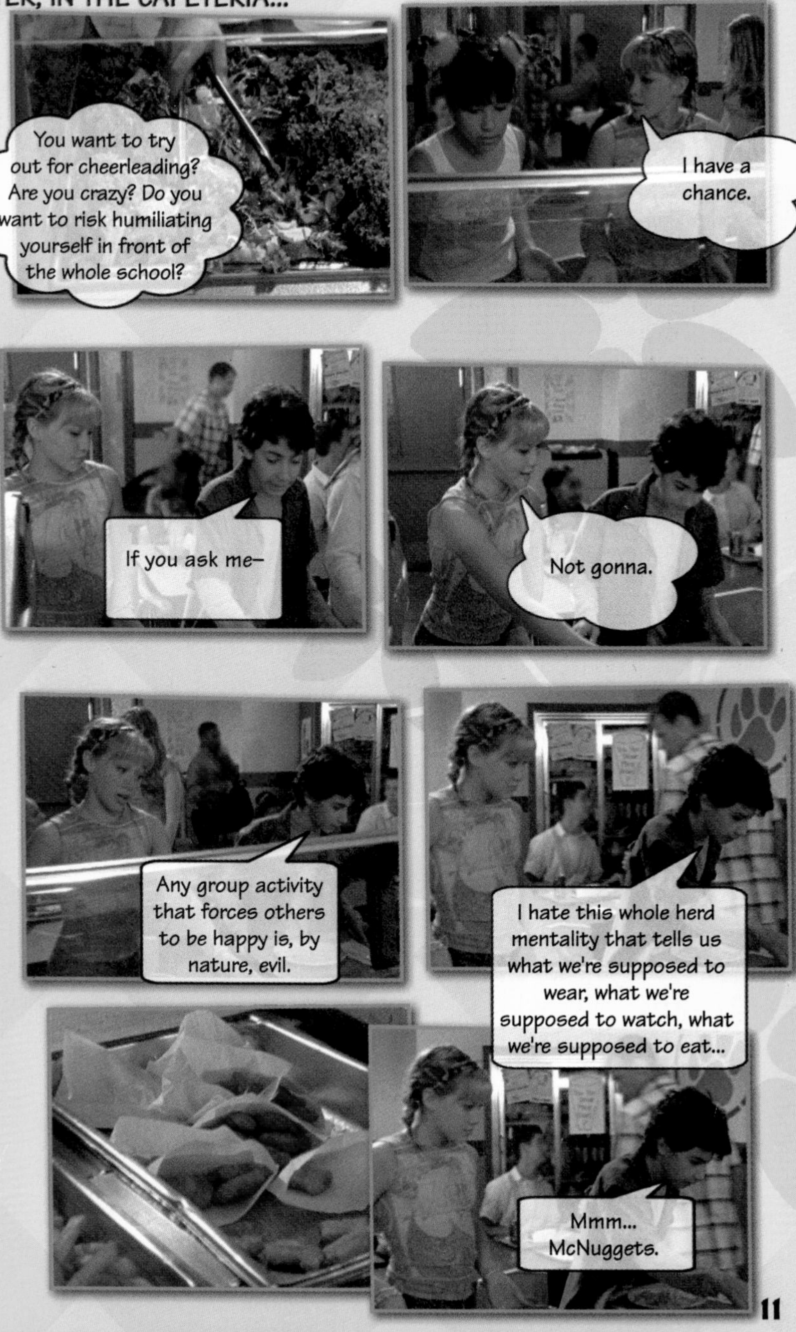
You want to try out for cheerleading? Are you crazy? Do you want to risk humiliating yourself in front of the whole school?
I have a chance.
If you ask me–
Not gonna.
Any group activity that forces others to be happy is, by nature, evil.
I hate this whole herd mentality that tells us what we're supposed to wear, what we're supposed to watch, what we're supposed to eat...
Mmm... McNuggets.

AFTER SCHOOL IN THE GYM...

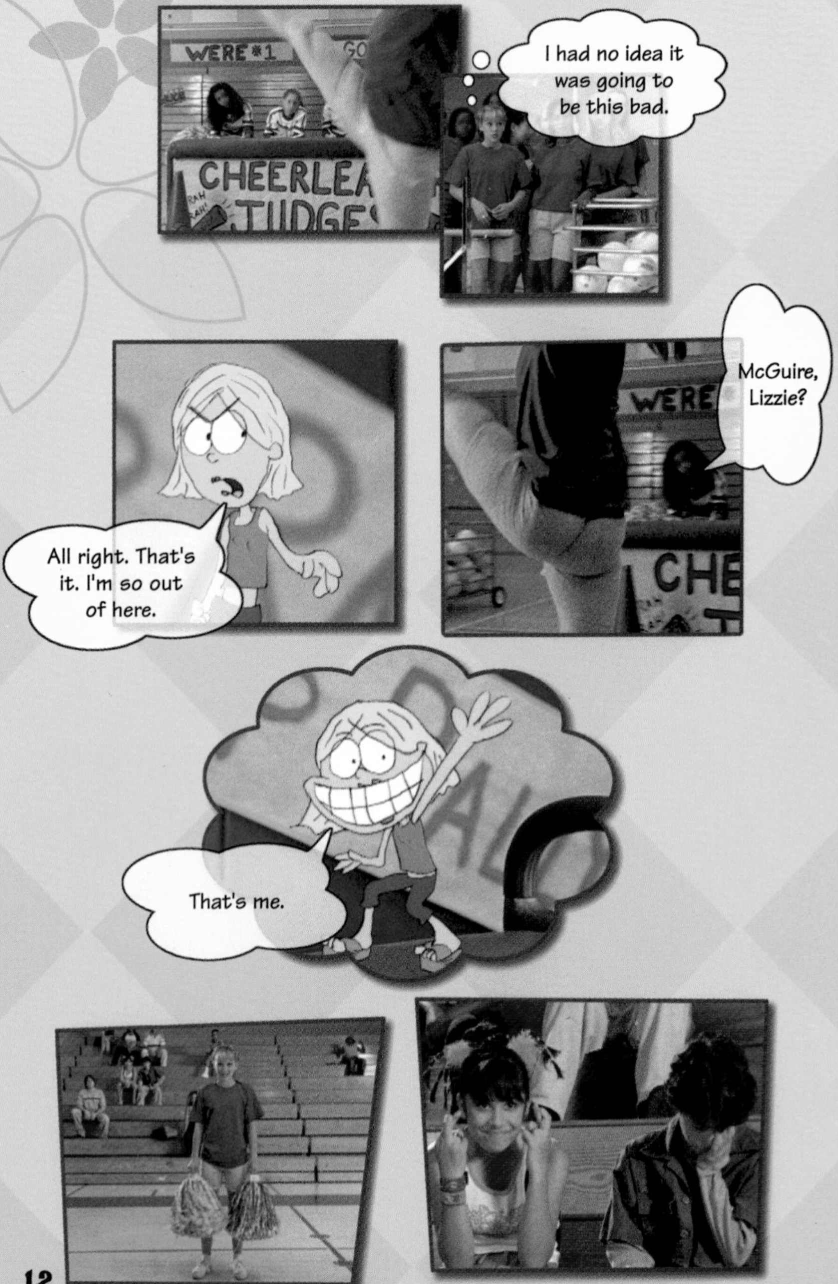
I had no idea it was going to be this bad.
All right. That's it. I'm so out of here.
McGuire, Lizzie?
That's me.

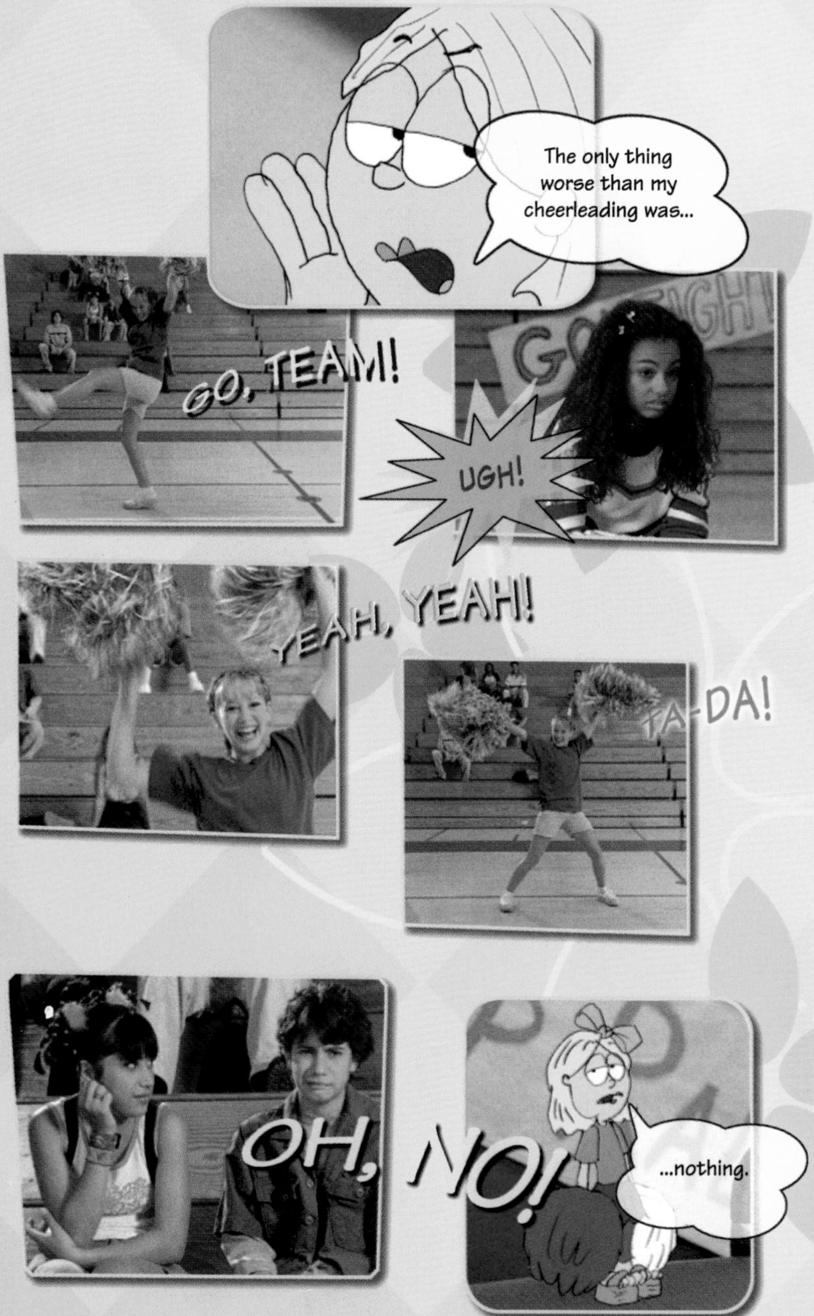
The only thing worse than my cheerleading was...
GO, TEAM!
UGH!
YEAH, YEAH!
TA-DA!
OH, NO!
...nothing.

BACK AT HOME...

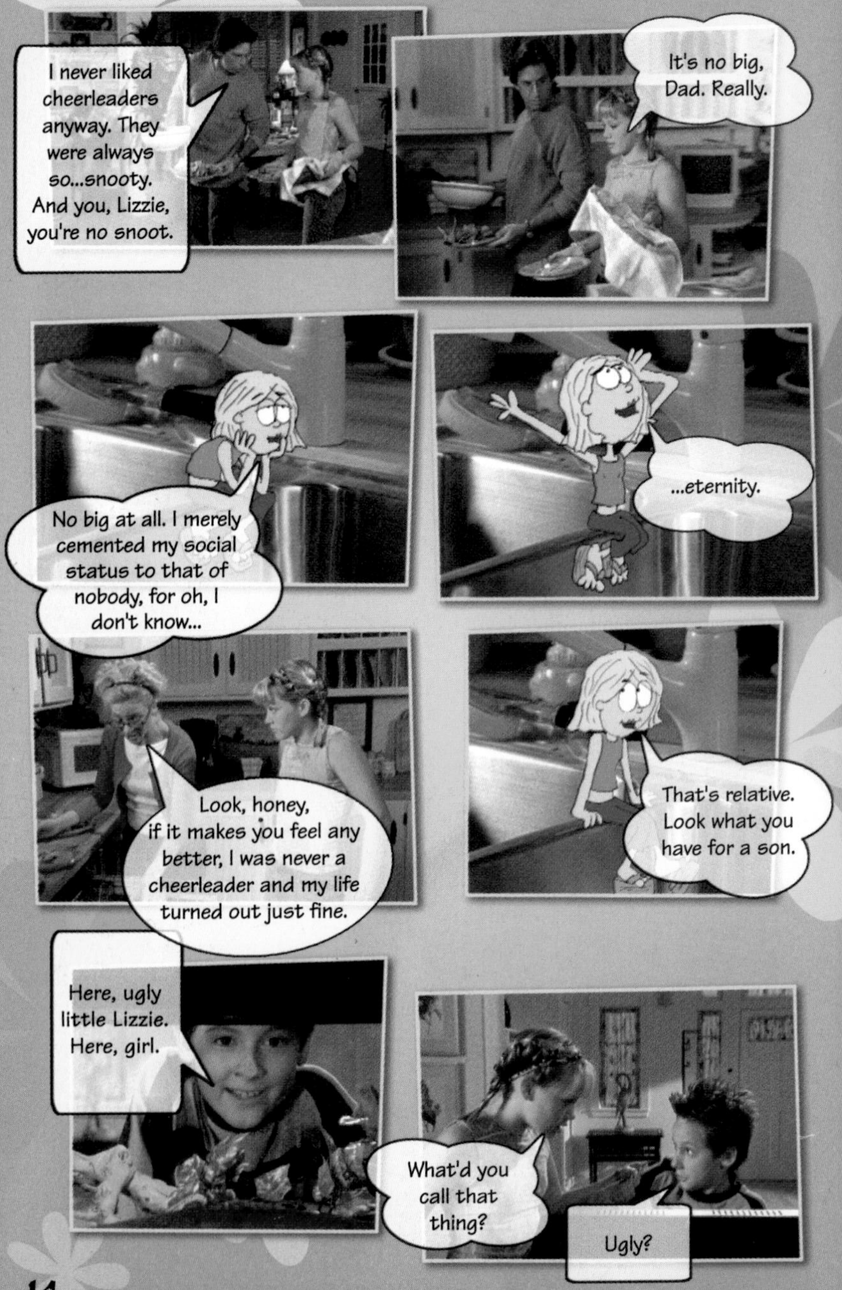
I never liked cheerleaders anyway. They were always so...snooty. And you, Lizzie, you're no snoot.
It's no big, Dad. Really.
No big at all. I merely cemented my social status to that of nobody, for oh, I don't know...
...eternity.
Look, honey, if it makes you feel any better, I was never a cheerleader and my life turned out just fine.
That's relative. Look what you have for a son.
Here, ugly little Lizzie. Here, girl.
What'd you call that thing?
Ugly?

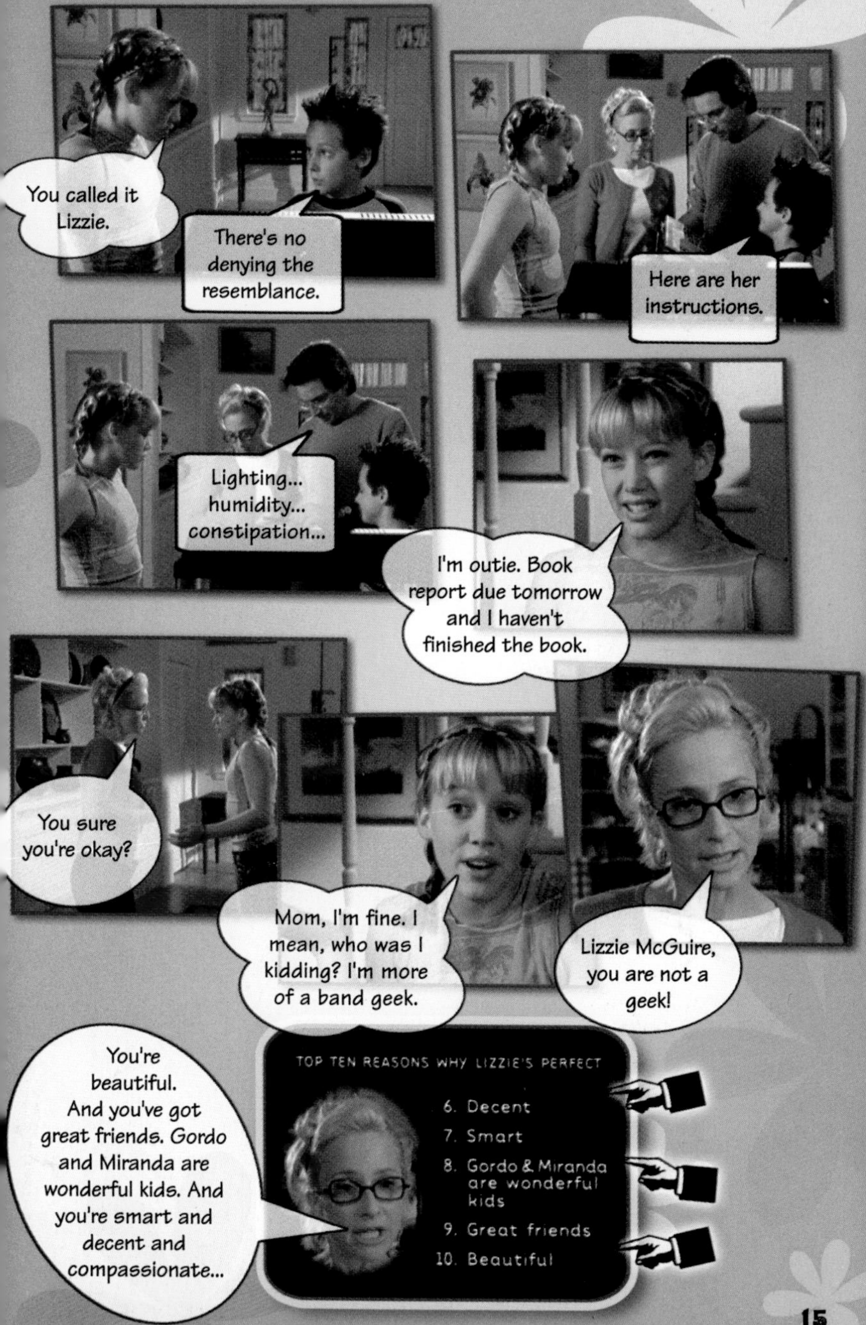
You called it Lizzie.
There's no denying the resemblance.
Here are her instructions.
Lighting... humidity... constipation...
I'm outie. Book report due tomorrow and I haven't finished the book.
You sure you're okay?
Mom, I'm fine. I mean, who was I kidding? I'm more of a band geek.
Lizzie McGuire, you are not a geek!
You're beautiful. And you've got great friends. Gordo and Miranda are wonderful kids. And you're smart and decent and compassionate...
TOP TEN REASONS WHY LIZZIE'S PERFECT
6. Decent
7. Smart
8. Gordo & Miranda are wonderful kids
9. Great friends
10. Beautiful

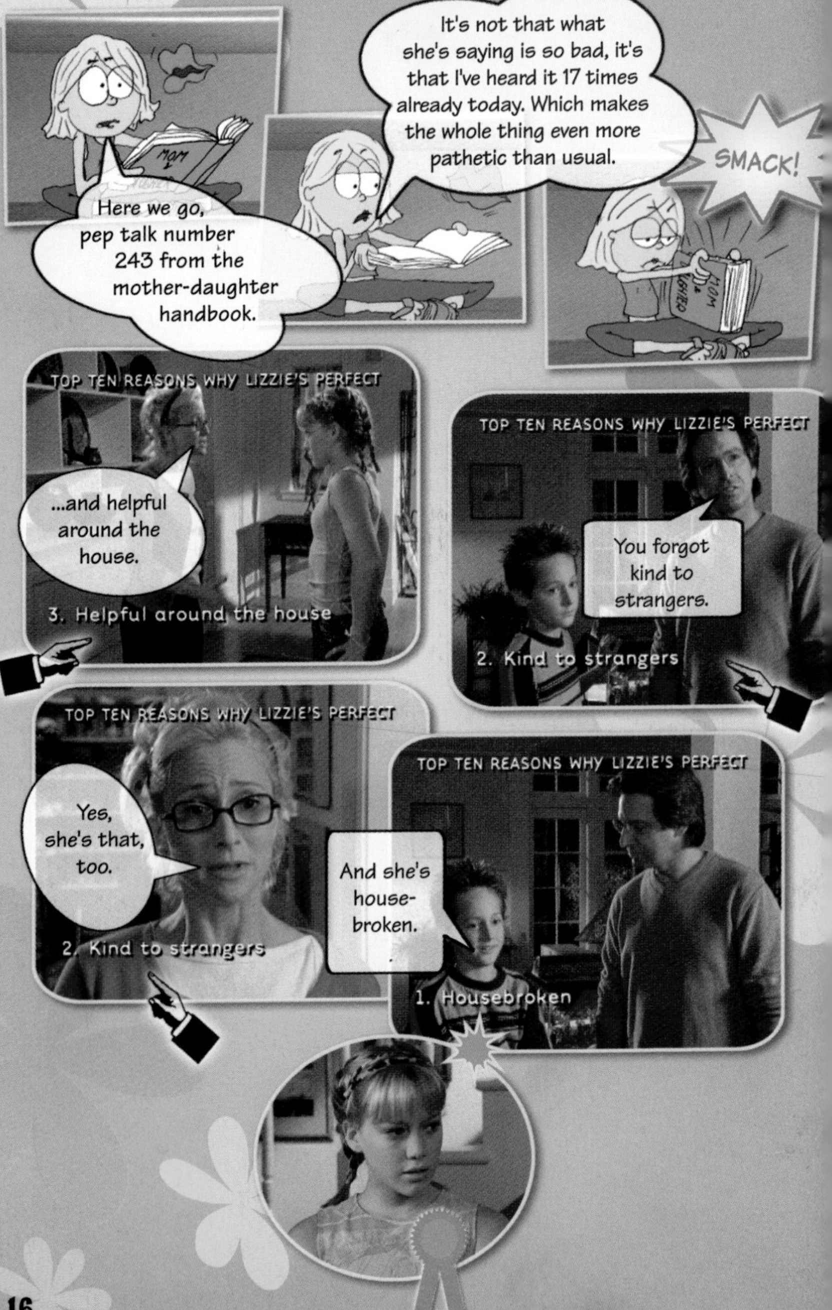
MOM
Here we go, pep talk number 243 from the mother-daughter handbook.
It's not that what she's saying is so bad, it's that I've heard it 17 times already today. Which makes the whole thing even more pathetic than usual.
SMACK!
TOP TEN REASONS WHY LIZZIE'S PERFECT
...and helpful around the house.
3. Helpful around the house
TOP TEN REASONS WHY LIZZIE'S PERFECT
You forgot kind to strangers.
2. Kind to strangers
TOP TEN REASONS WHY LIZZIE'S PERFECT
Yes, she's that, too.
2. Kind to strangers
TOP TEN REASONS WHY LIZZIE'S PERFECT
And she's house-broken.
1. Housebroken

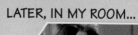

DING! DING!

Miranda.

I'm telling you now to avoid major devastation tomorrow...

TAP

TAP

MessageFRM

Current session with: MANDER (online
MANDER: I'm telling you now to avoid me
MANDER: Kate made cheerleader

Kate made cheerleader.

CLICK

TAP

You know why she made it, don't you?

Messagerrm

Current session with: MANDER (online
MANDER: I'm telling you now to avoid me
MANDER: Kate made cheerleade
You know why she made it
MANDER: Why?

Why?

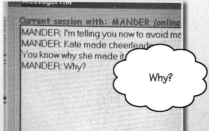

17

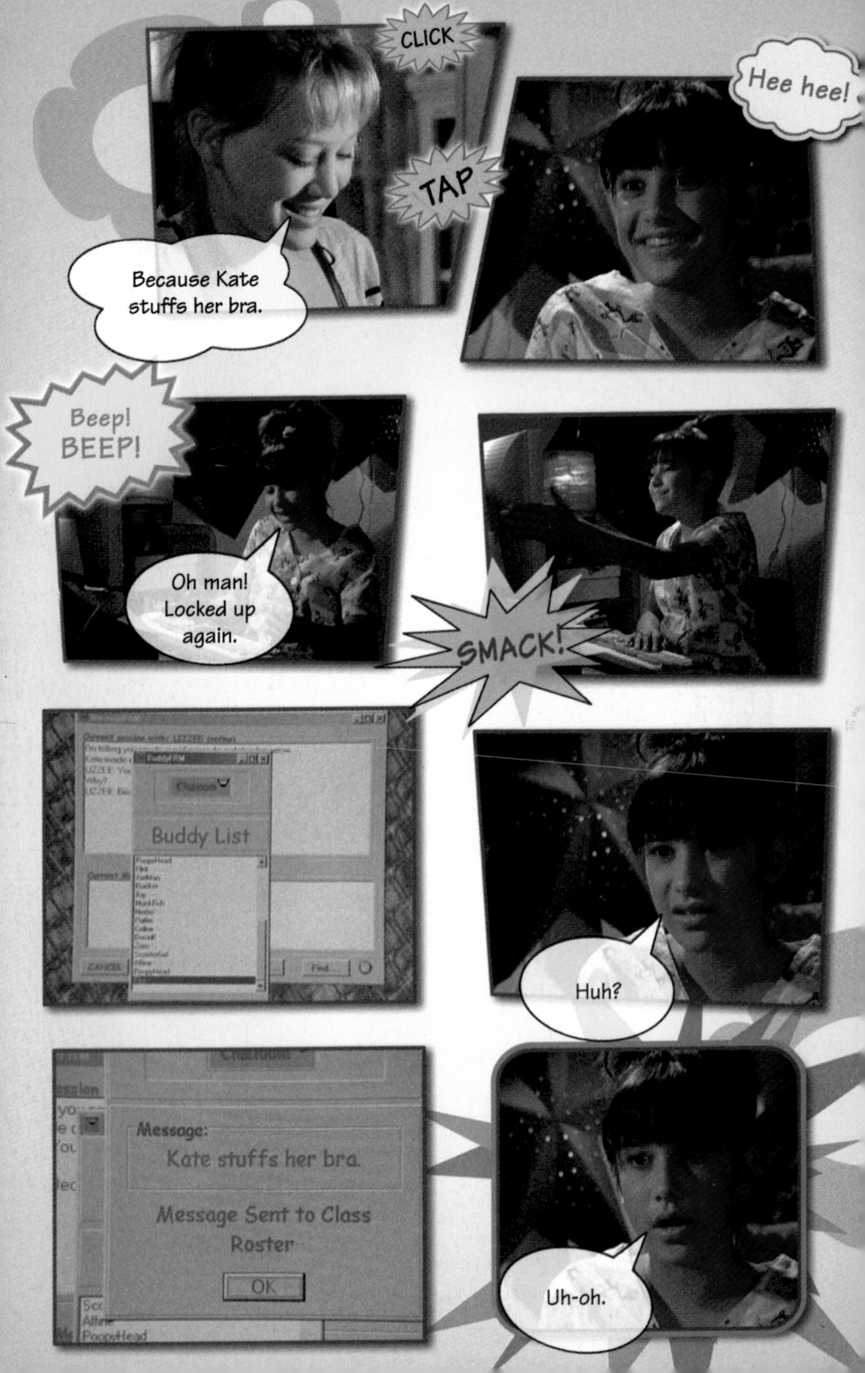
CLICK
Because Kate stuffs her bra.
TAP
Hee hee!
Beep! BEEP!
Oh man! Locked up again.
SMACK!
Buddy List
CANCEL
Find...
Huh?
Message:
Kate stuffs her bra.
Message Sent to Class Roster
OK
Uh-oh.

THE NEXT DAY AT SCHOOL...

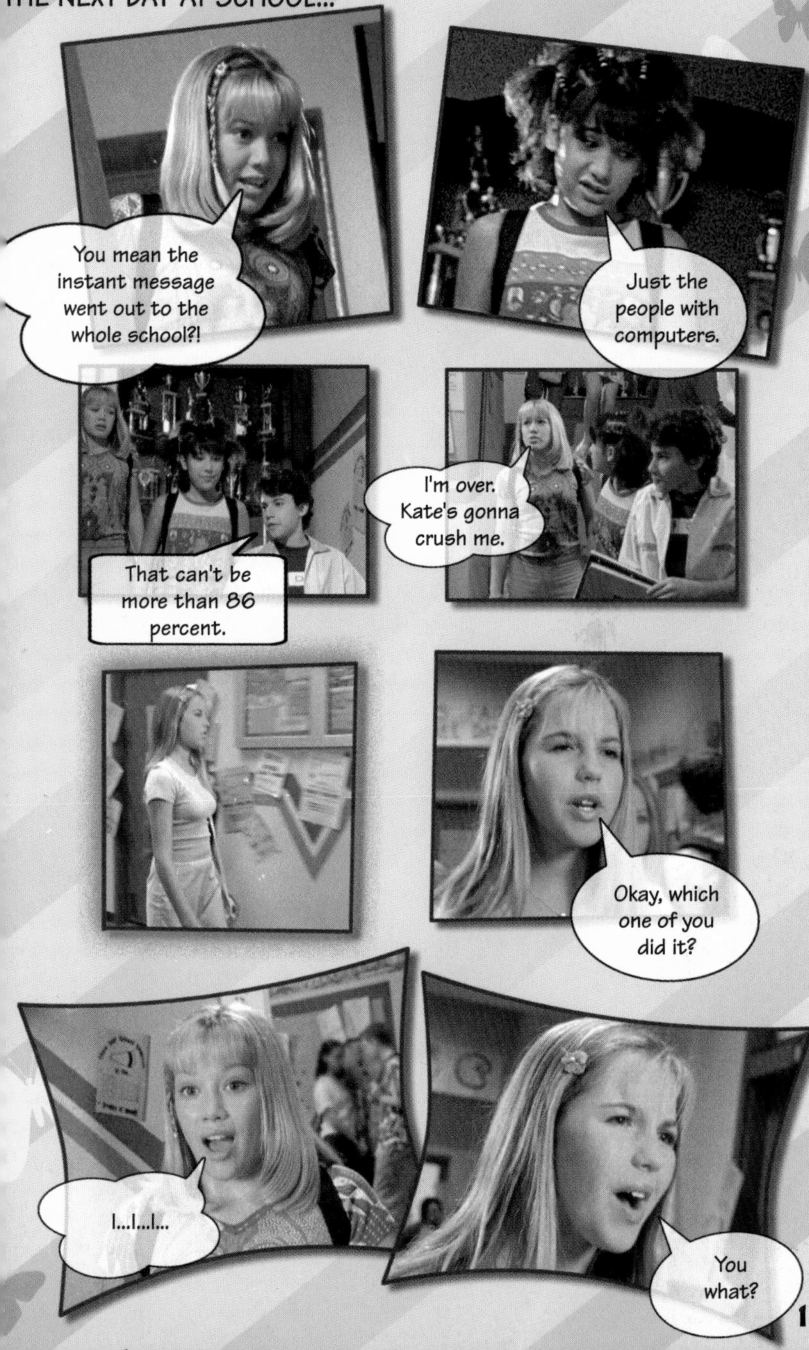
You mean the instant message went out to the whole school?!
Just the people with computers.
That can't be more than 86 percent.
I'm over. Kate's gonna crush me.
Okay, which one of you did it?
I...I...I...
You what?

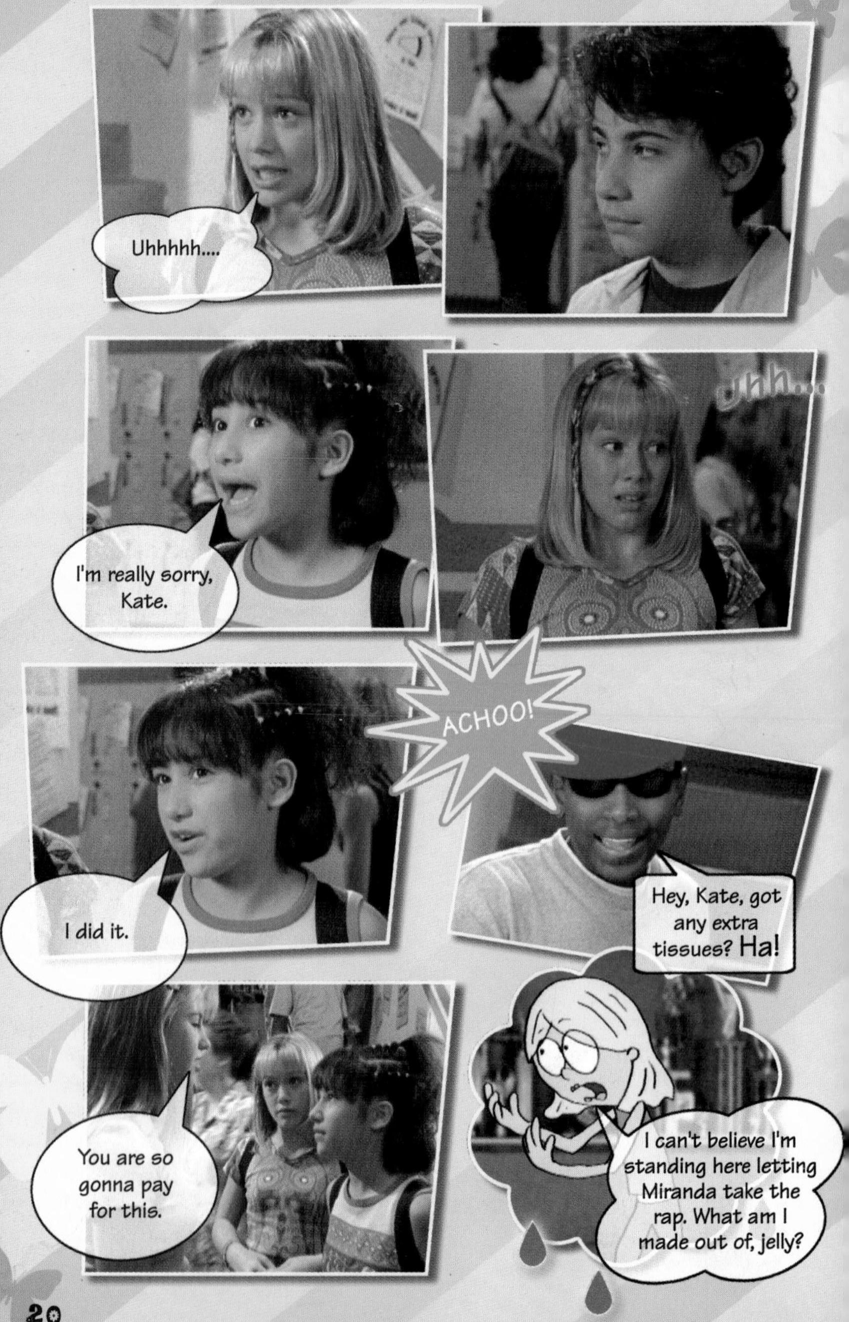
Uhhhhh....
I'm really sorry, Kate.
Uhh...
I did it.
ACHOO!
Hey, Kate, got any extra tissues? Ha!
You are so gonna pay for this.
I can't believe I'm standing here letting Miranda take the rap. What am I made out of, jelly?

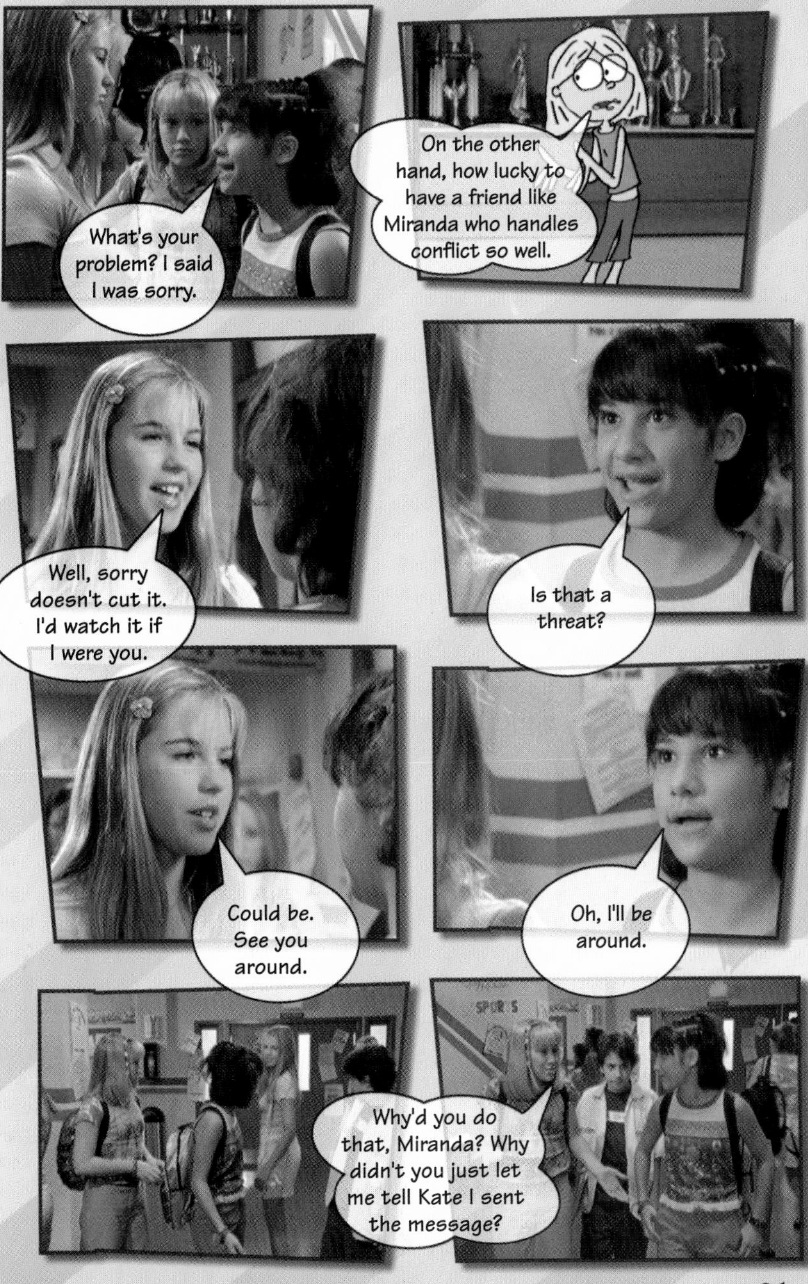
What's your problem? I said I was sorry.
On the other hand, how lucky to have a friend like Miranda who handles conflict so well.
Well, sorry doesn't cut it. I'd watch it if I were you.
Is that a threat?
Could be. See you around.
Oh, I'll be around.
Why'd you do that, Miranda? Why didn't you just let me tell Kate I sent the message?

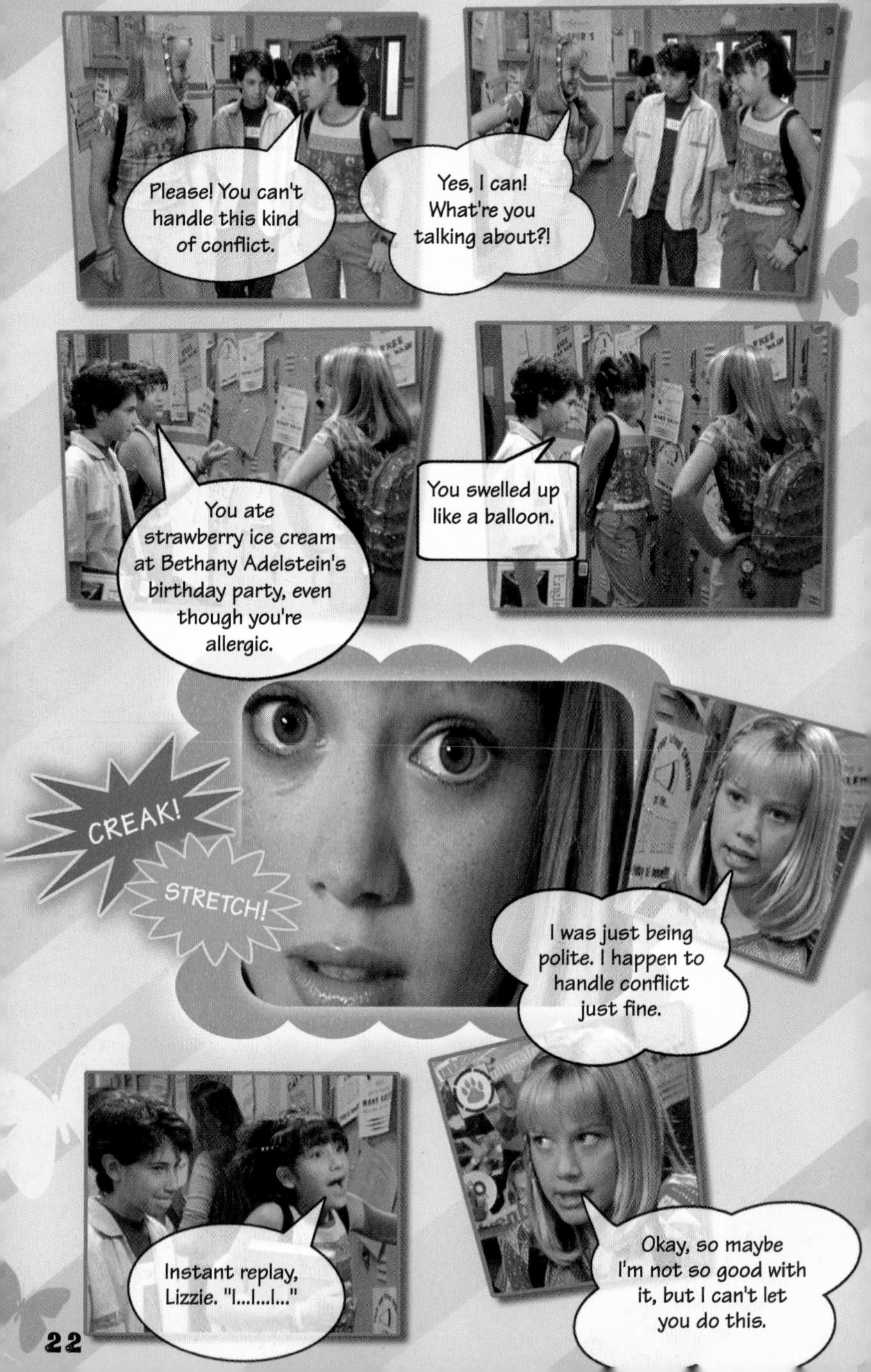
Please! You can't handle this kind of conflict.
Yes, I can! What're you talking about?!
You ate strawberry ice cream at Bethany Adelstein's birthday party, even though you're allergic.
You swelled up like a balloon.
CREAK!
STRETCH!
I was just being polite. I happen to handle conflict just fine.
Instant replay, Lizzie. "I...I...I..."
Okay, so maybe I'm not so good with it, but I can't let you do this.

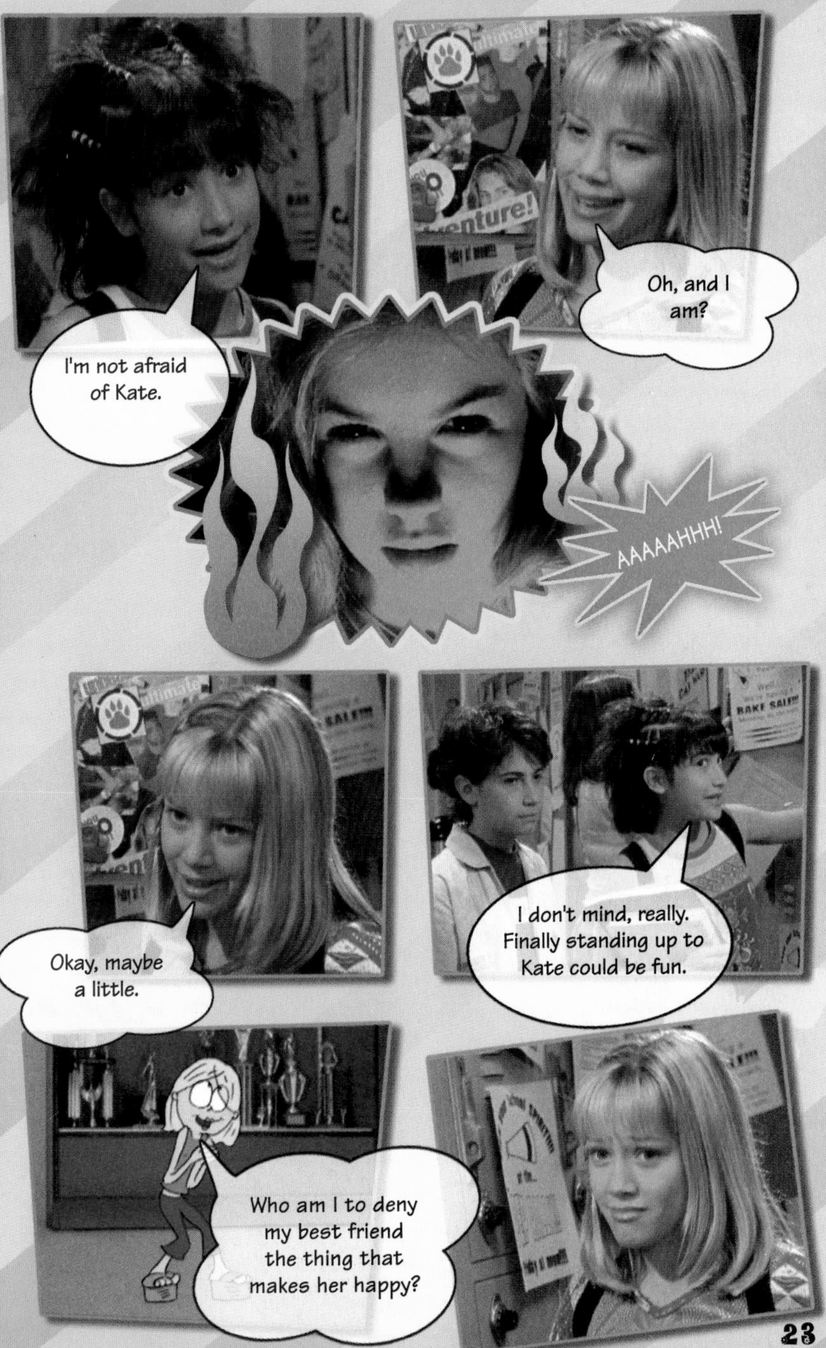
I'm not afraid of Kate.
Oh, and I am?
AAAAHHH!
Okay, maybe a little.
I don't mind, really. Finally standing up to Kate could be fun.
Who am I to deny my best friend the thing that makes her happy?

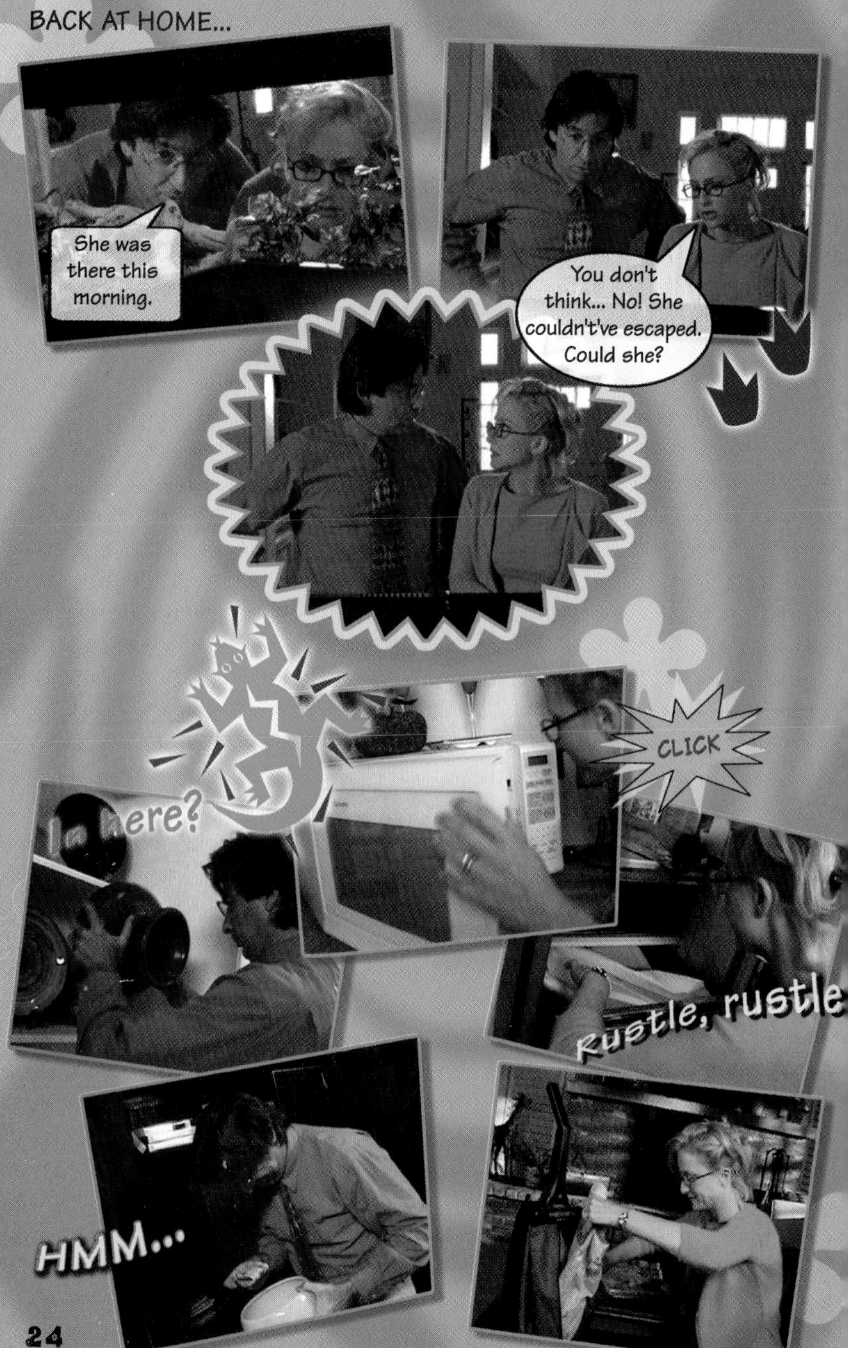
BACK AT HOME...
She was there this morning.
You don't think... No! She couldn't've escaped. Could she?
here?
CLICK
Rustle, rustle
HMM...

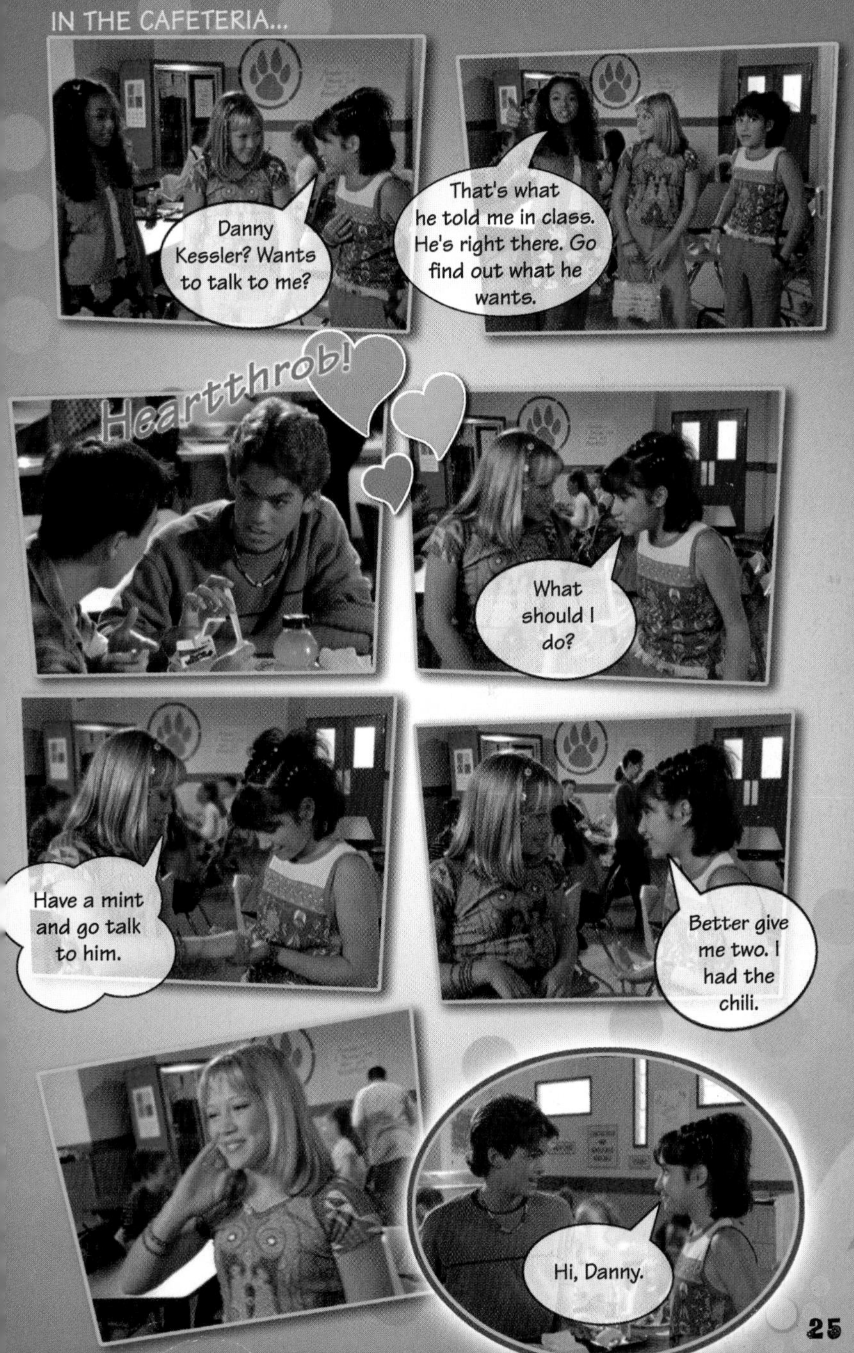
IN THE CAFETERIA...
Danny Kessler? Wants to talk to me?
That's what he told me in class. He's right there. Go find out what he wants.
Heartthrob!
What should I do?
Have a mint and go talk to him.
Better give me two. I had the chili.
Hi, Danny.

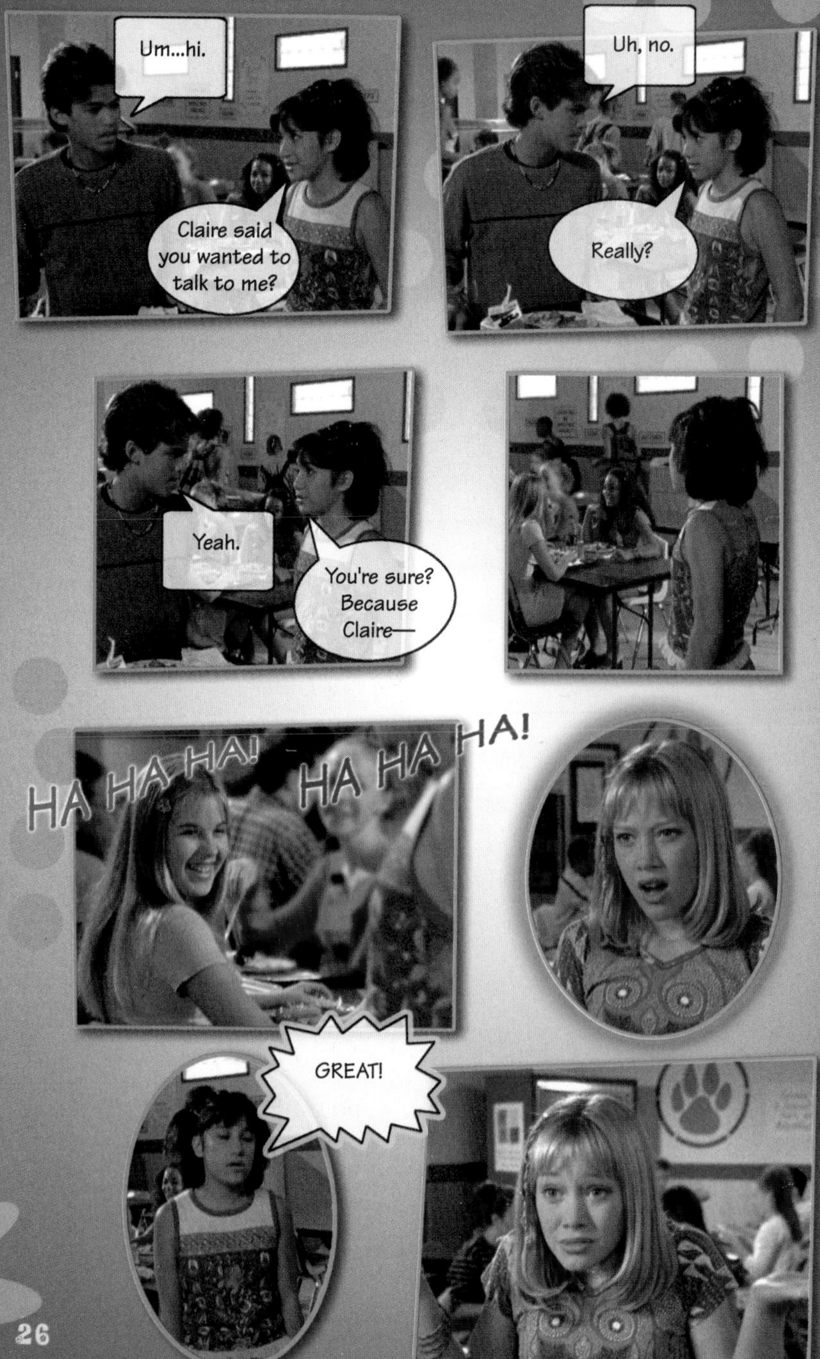
Um...hi.
Claire said you wanted to talk to me?
Uh, no.
Really?
Yeah.
You're sure? Because Claire—
HA HA HA!
HA HA HA!
GREAT!

AT HOME AGAIN...

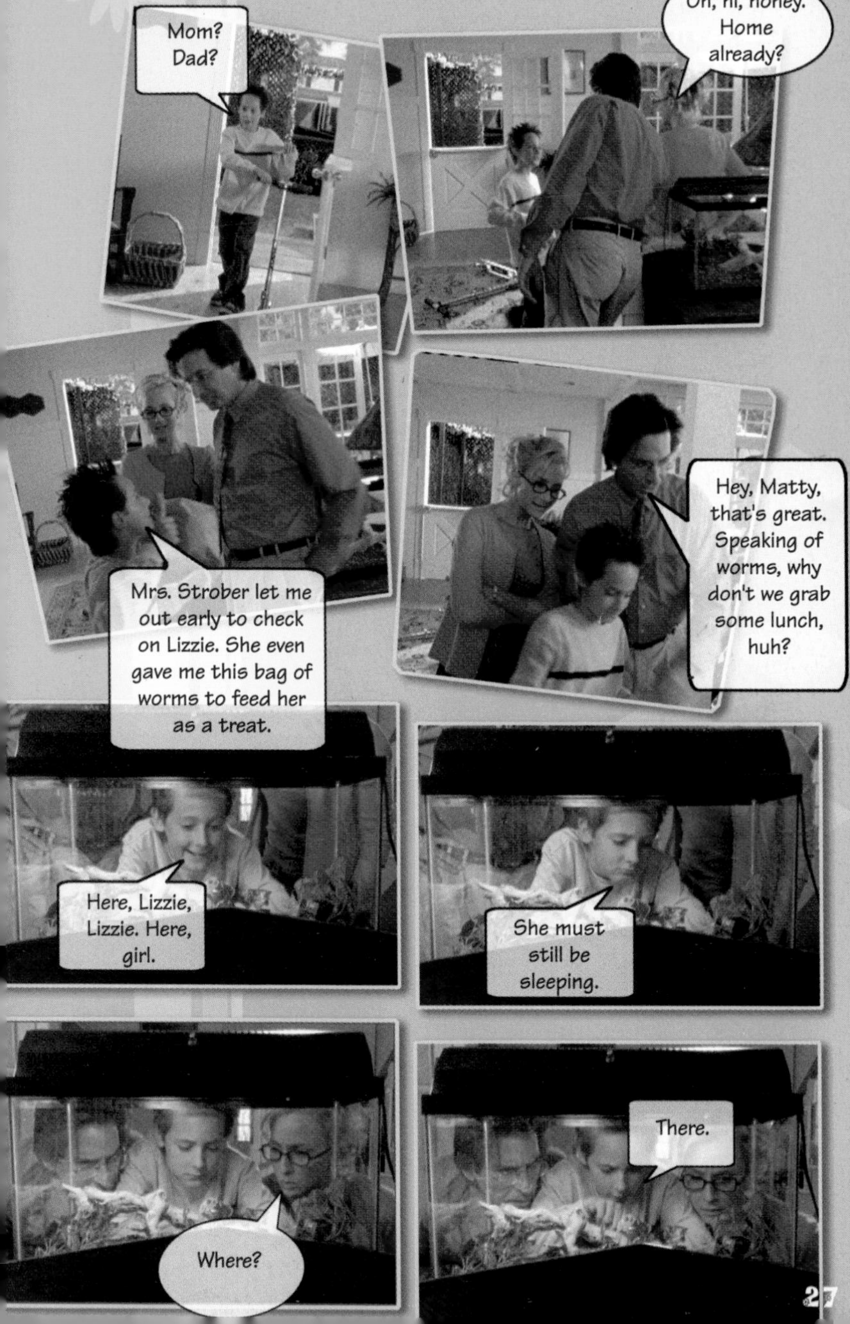
Mom? Dad?
Oh, hi, honey. Home already?
Mrs. Strober let me out early to check on Lizzie. She even gave me this bag of worms to feed her as a treat.
Hey, Matty, that's great. Speaking of worms, why don't we grab some lunch, huh?
Here, Lizzie, Lizzie. Here, girl.
She must still be sleeping.
Where?
There.

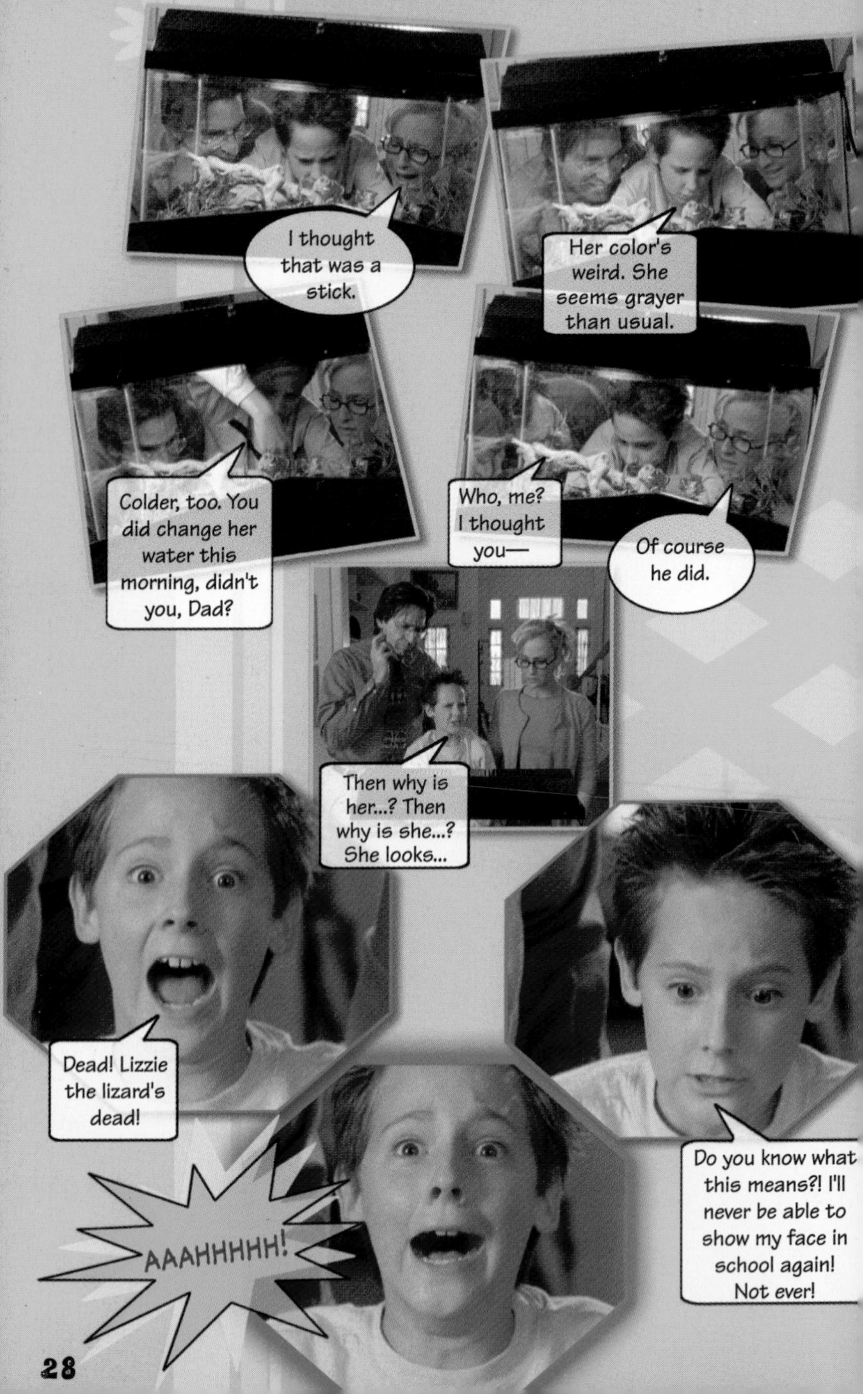
I thought that was a stick.
Her color's weird. She seems grayer than usual.
Colder, too. You did change her water this morning, didn't you, Dad?
Who, me? I thought you—
Of course he did.
Then why is her...? Then why is she...? She looks...
Dead! Lizzie the lizard's dead!
Do you know what this means?! I'll never be able to show my face in school again! Not ever!
AAAHHHHH!

MEANWHILE, AT SCHOOL...

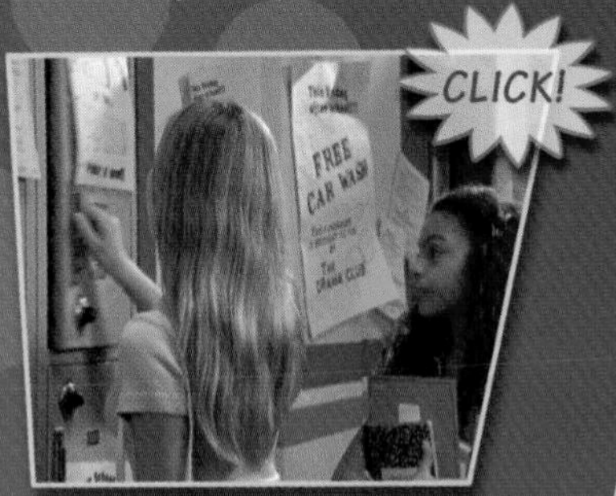
CLICK!
FREE CAR WASH

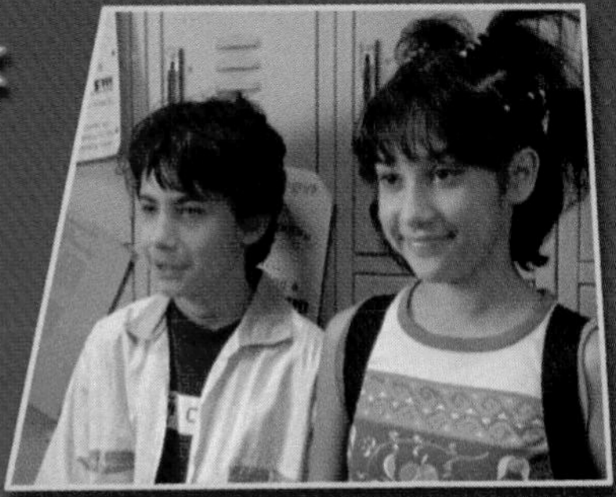

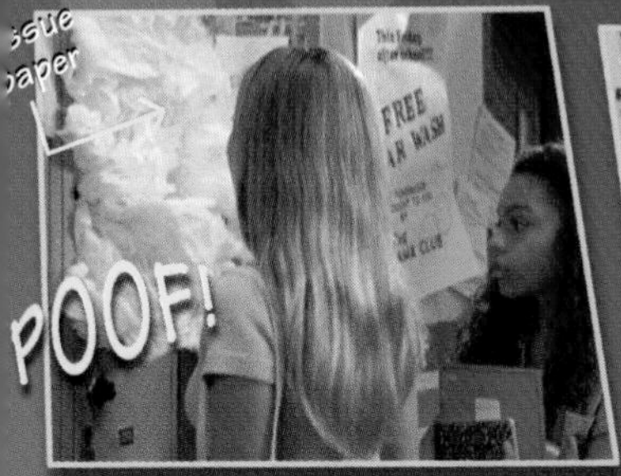
ssue
aper
FREE CAR WASH
POOF!

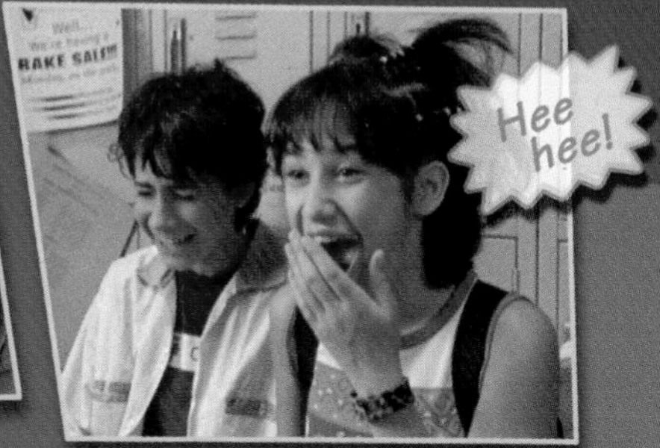
BAKE SALE!!!
Hee hee!

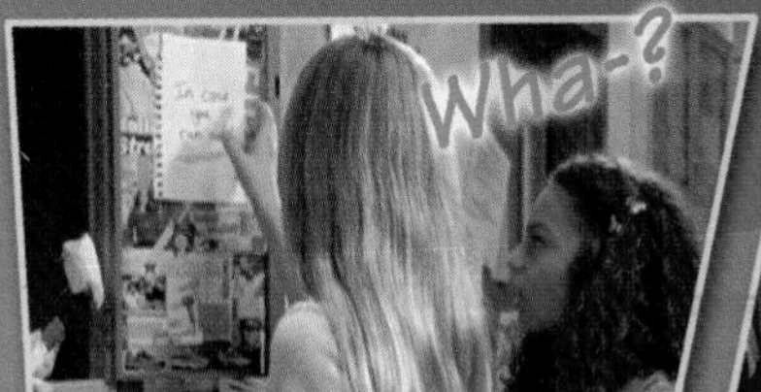
Wha-?

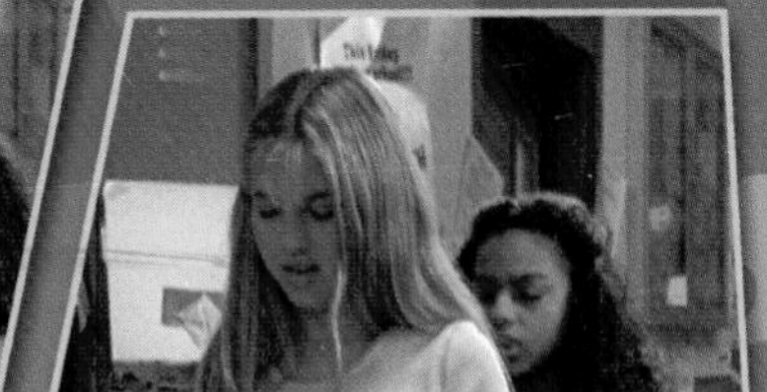

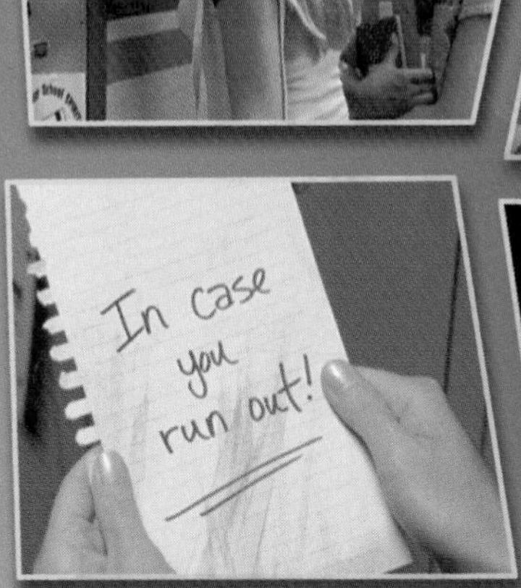
In case you run out!

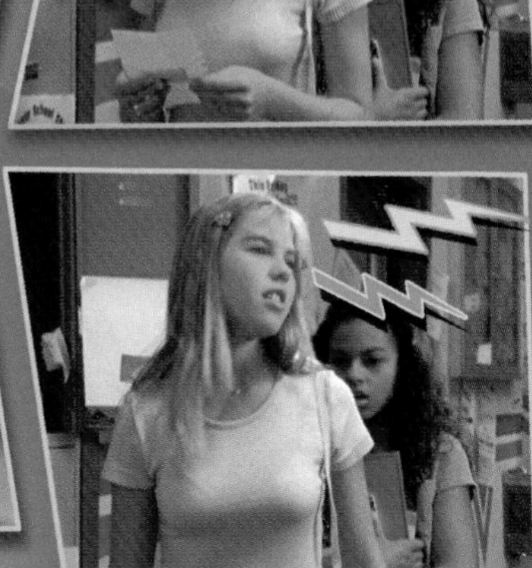

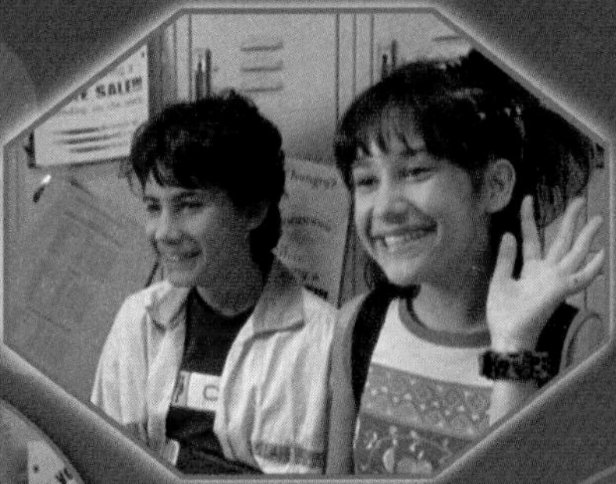

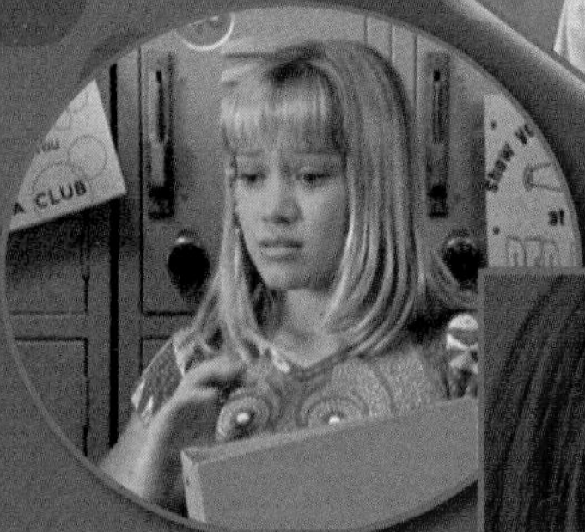

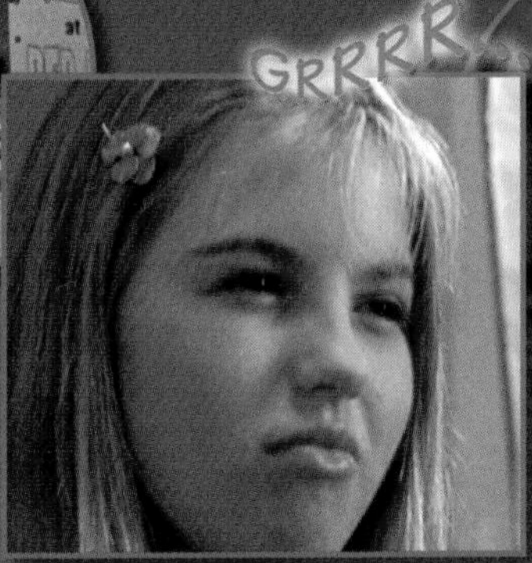
GRRRR

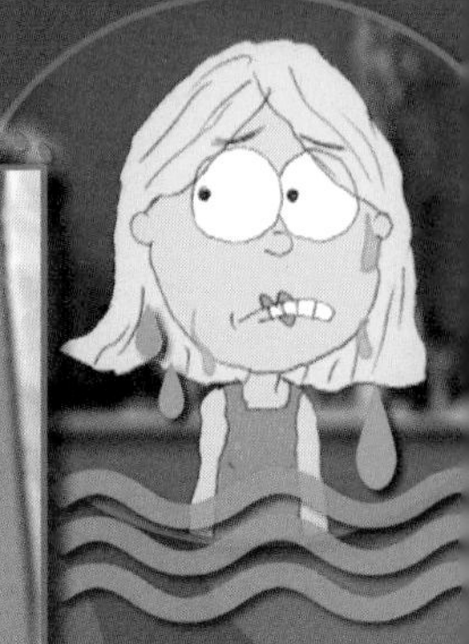

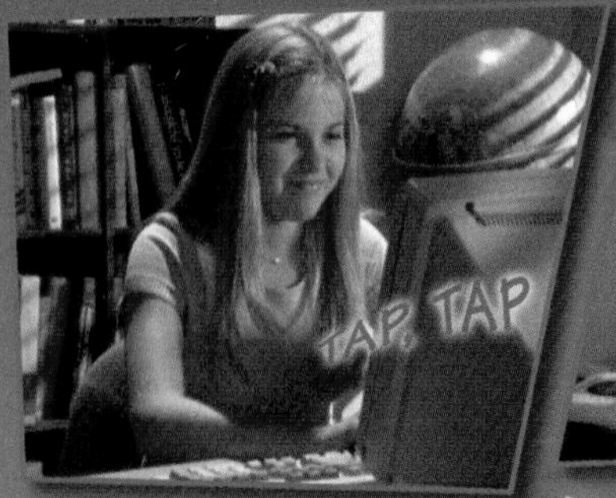
TAP, TAP

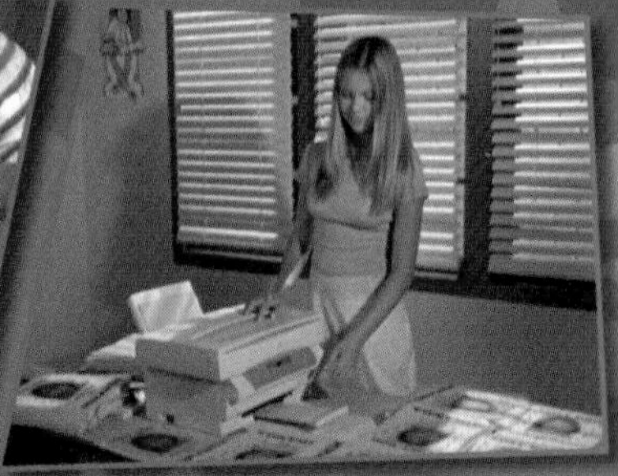

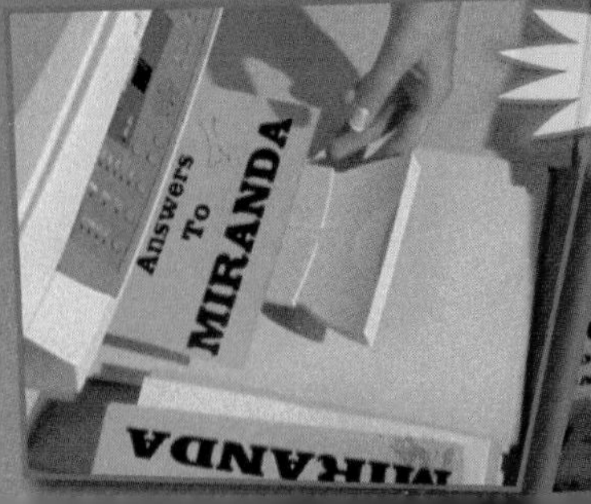
Answers
To
MIRANDA

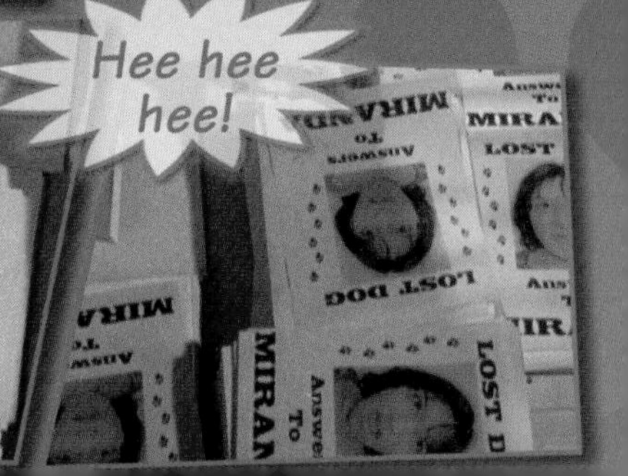
Hee hee
hee!
LOST DOG

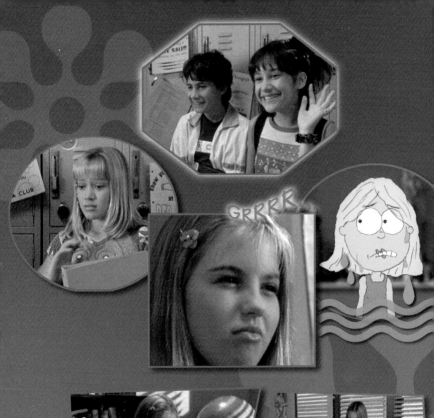

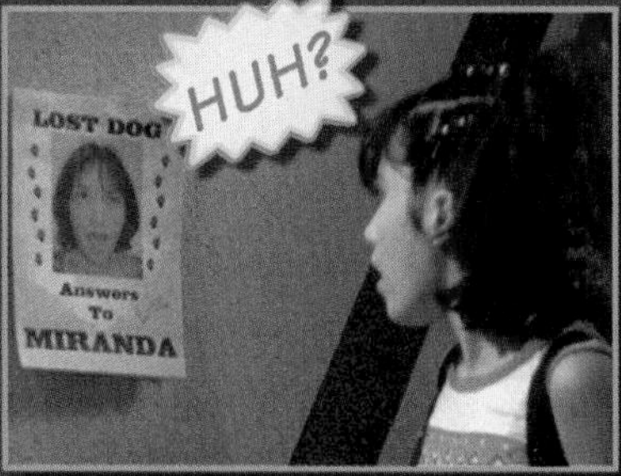
HUH?
LOST DOG
Answers To
MIRANDA

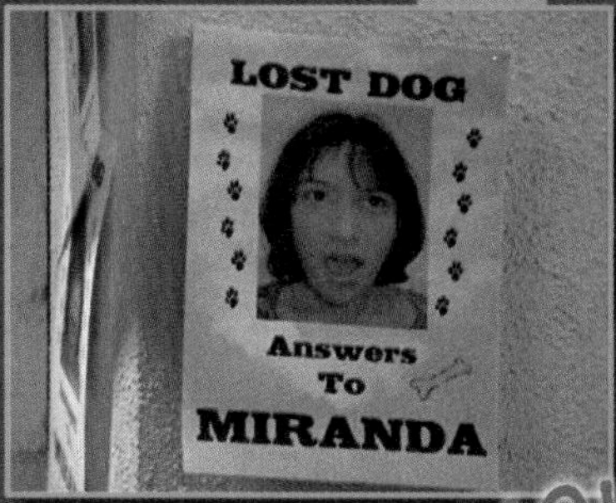
LOST DOG
Answers To
MIRANDA

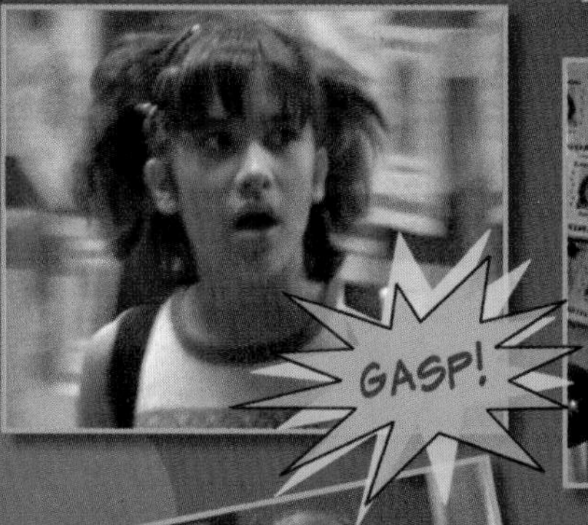
GASP!

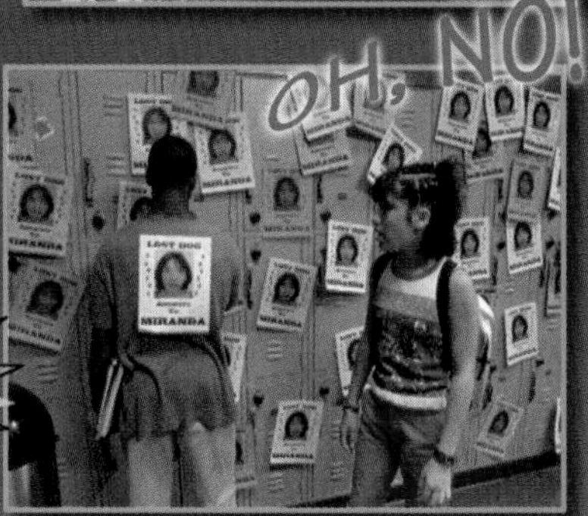
OH, NO!

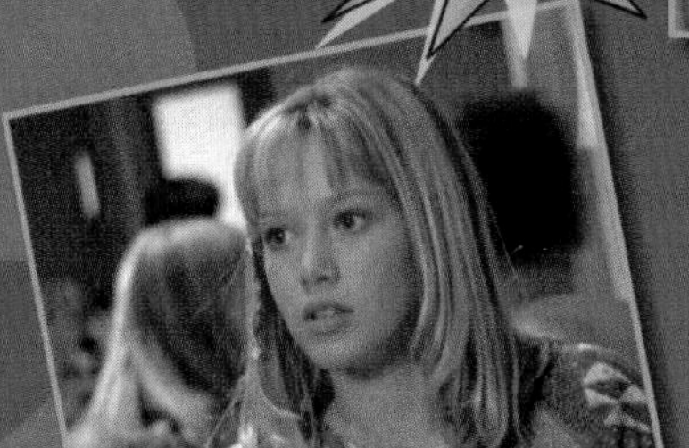

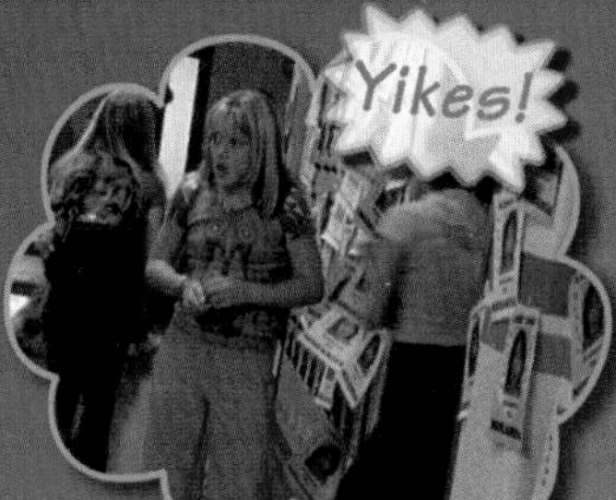
Yikes!

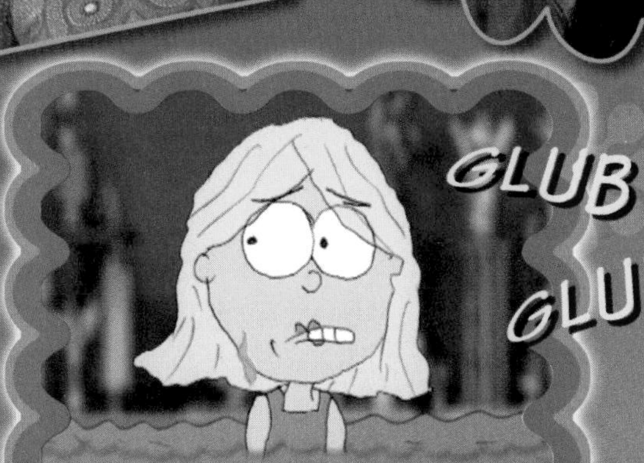
GLUB
GLUB

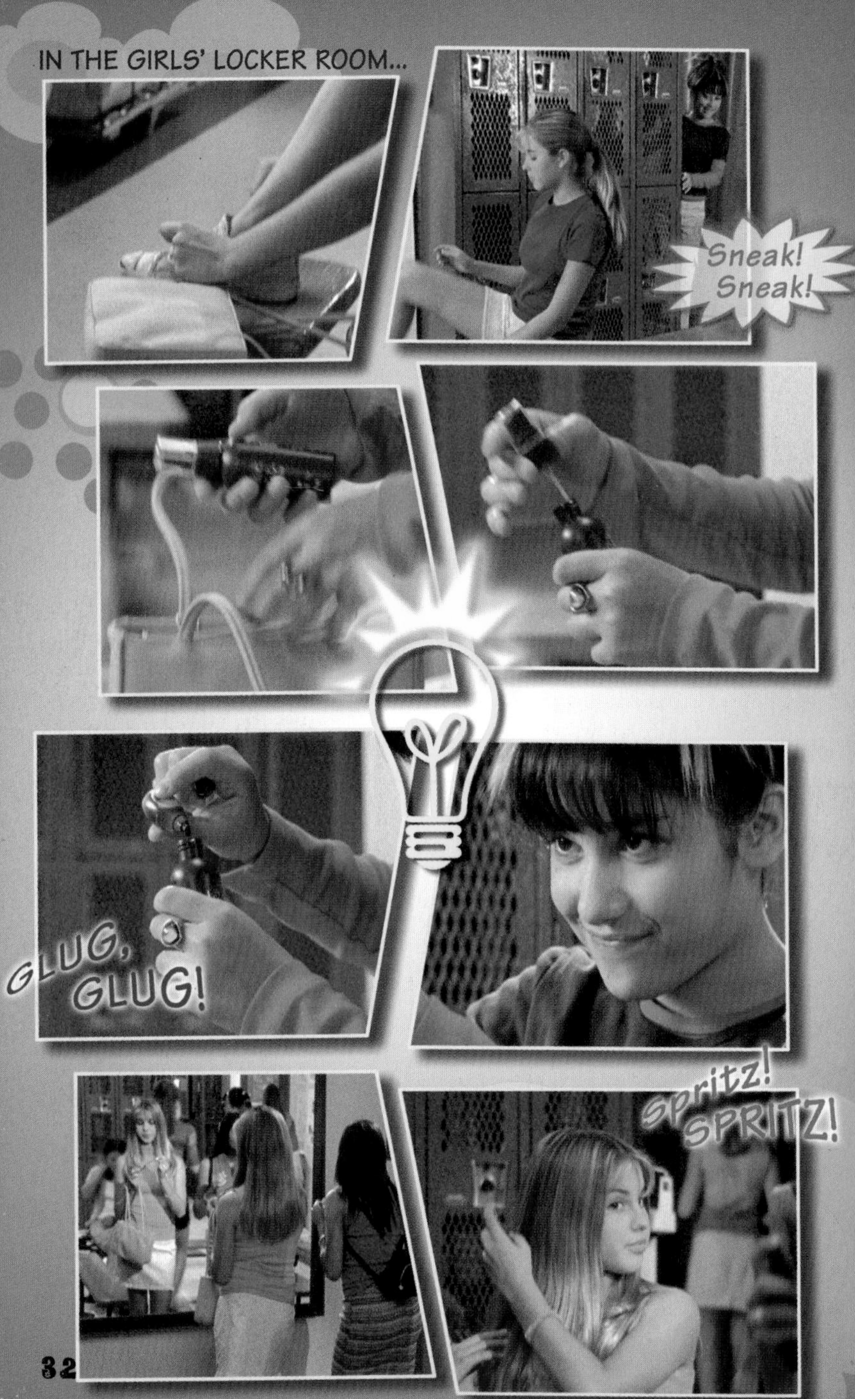
IN THE GIRLS' LOCKER ROOM...
Sneak! Sneak!
GLUG, GLUG!
Spritz! SPRITZ!

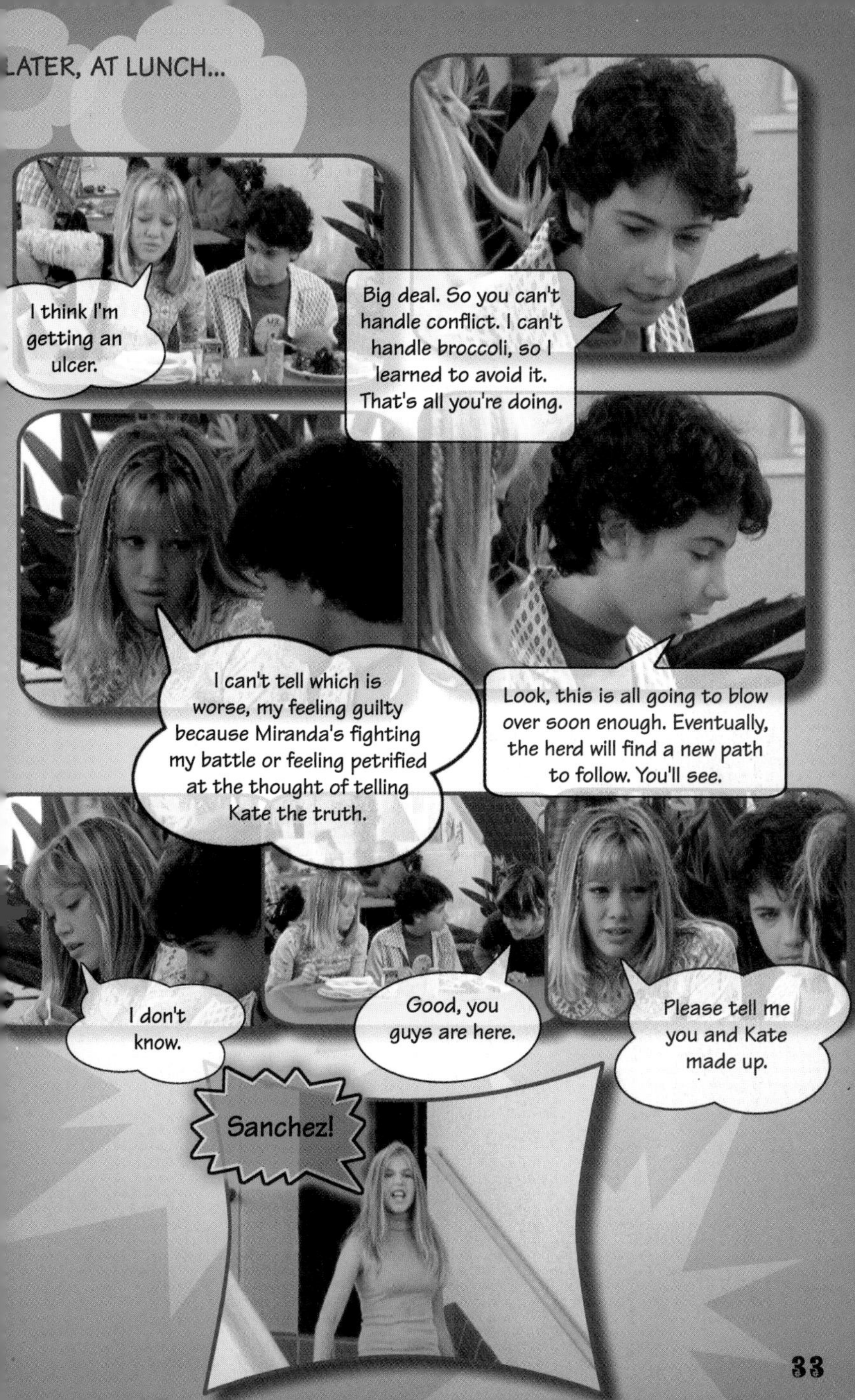
LATER, AT LUNCH...
I think I'm getting an ulcer.
Big deal. So you can't handle conflict. I can't handle broccoli, so I learned to avoid it. That's all you're doing.
I can't tell which is worse, my feeling guilty because Miranda's fighting my battle or feeling petrified at the thought of telling Kate the truth.
Look, this is all going to blow over soon enough. Eventually, the herd will find a new path to follow. You'll see.
I don't know.
Good, you guys are here.
Please tell me you and Kate made up.
Sanchez!

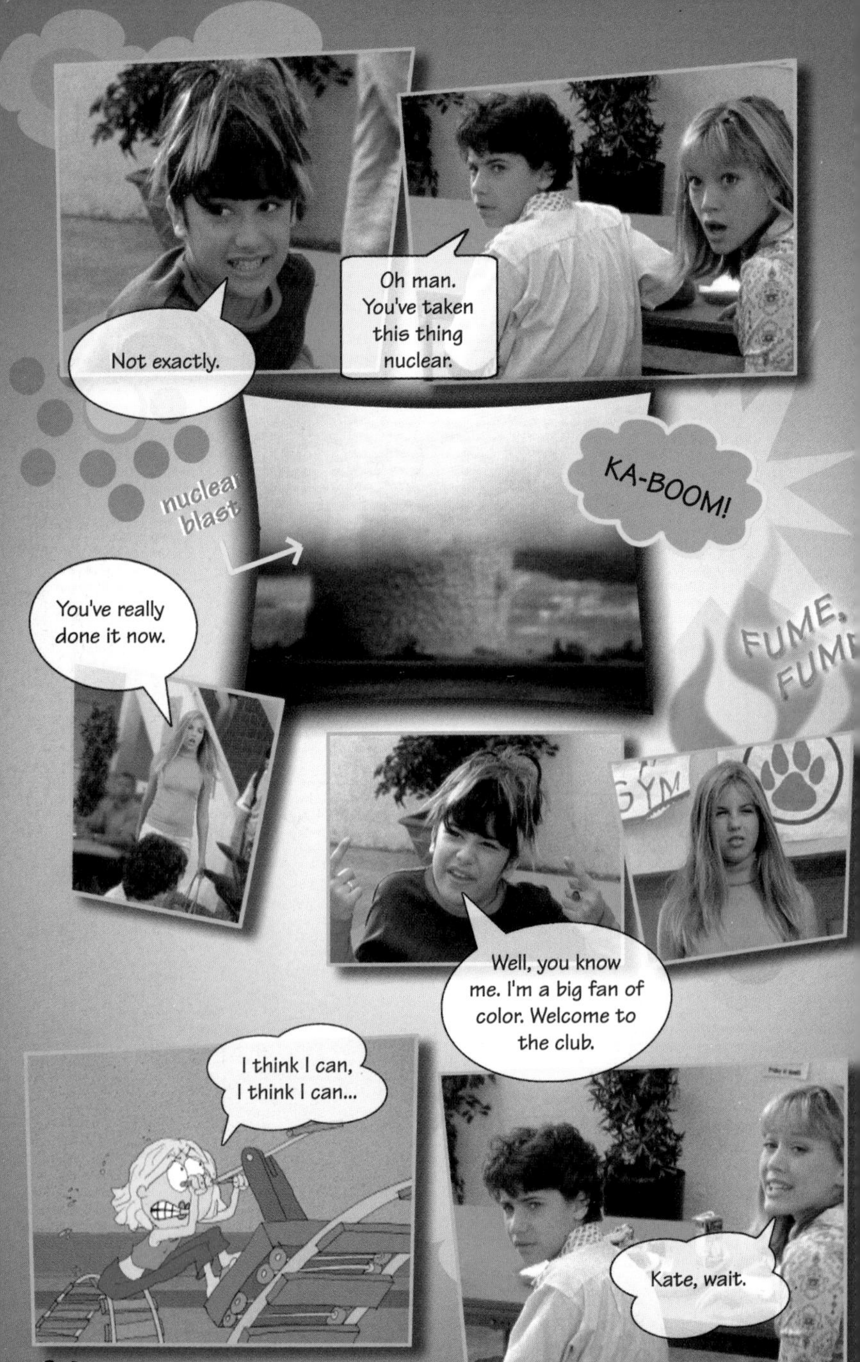
Not exactly.
Oh man. You've taken this thing nuclear.
nuclear blast
KA-BOOM!
You've really done it now.
FUME,
GYM
Well, you know me. I'm a big fan of color. Welcome to the club.
I think I can, I think I can...
Kate, wait.

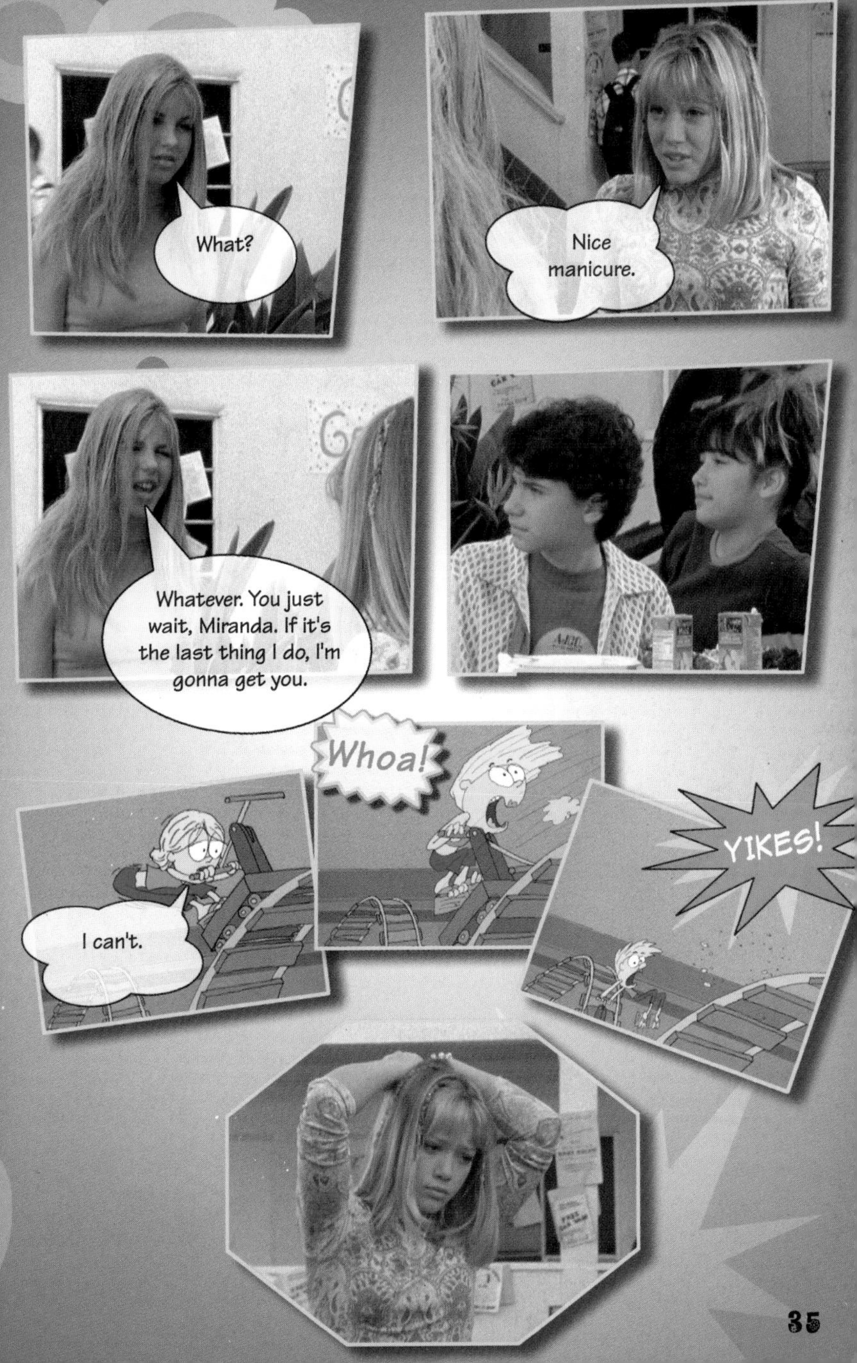
What?
Nice manicure.
Whatever. You just wait, Miranda. If it's the last thing I do, I'm gonna get you.
I can't.
Whoa!
YIKES!

THE NEXT DAY AT HOME...

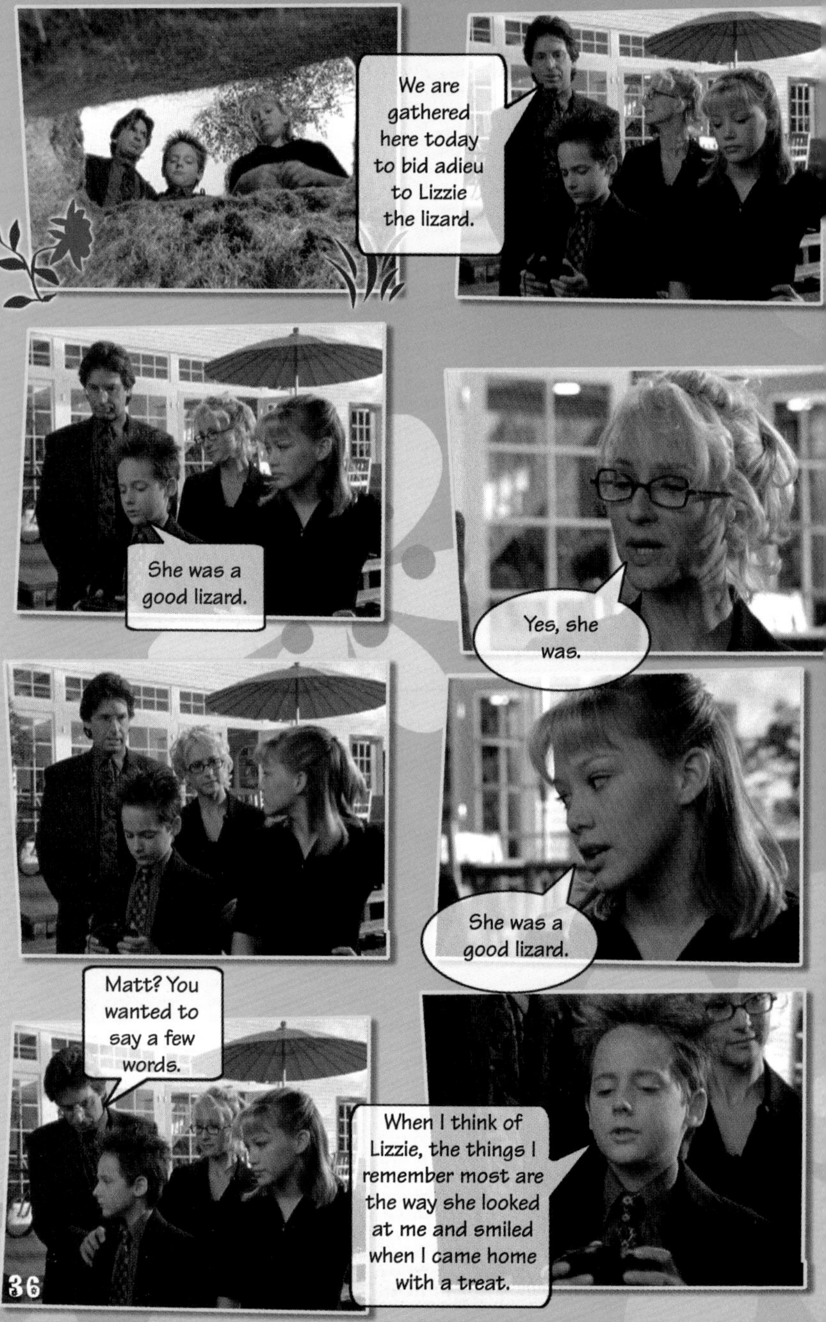

We are gathered here today to bid adieu to Lizzie the lizard.
She was a good lizard.
Yes, she was.
She was a good lizard.
Matt? You wanted to say a few words.
When I think of Lizzie, the things I remember most are the way she looked at me and smiled when I came home with a treat.

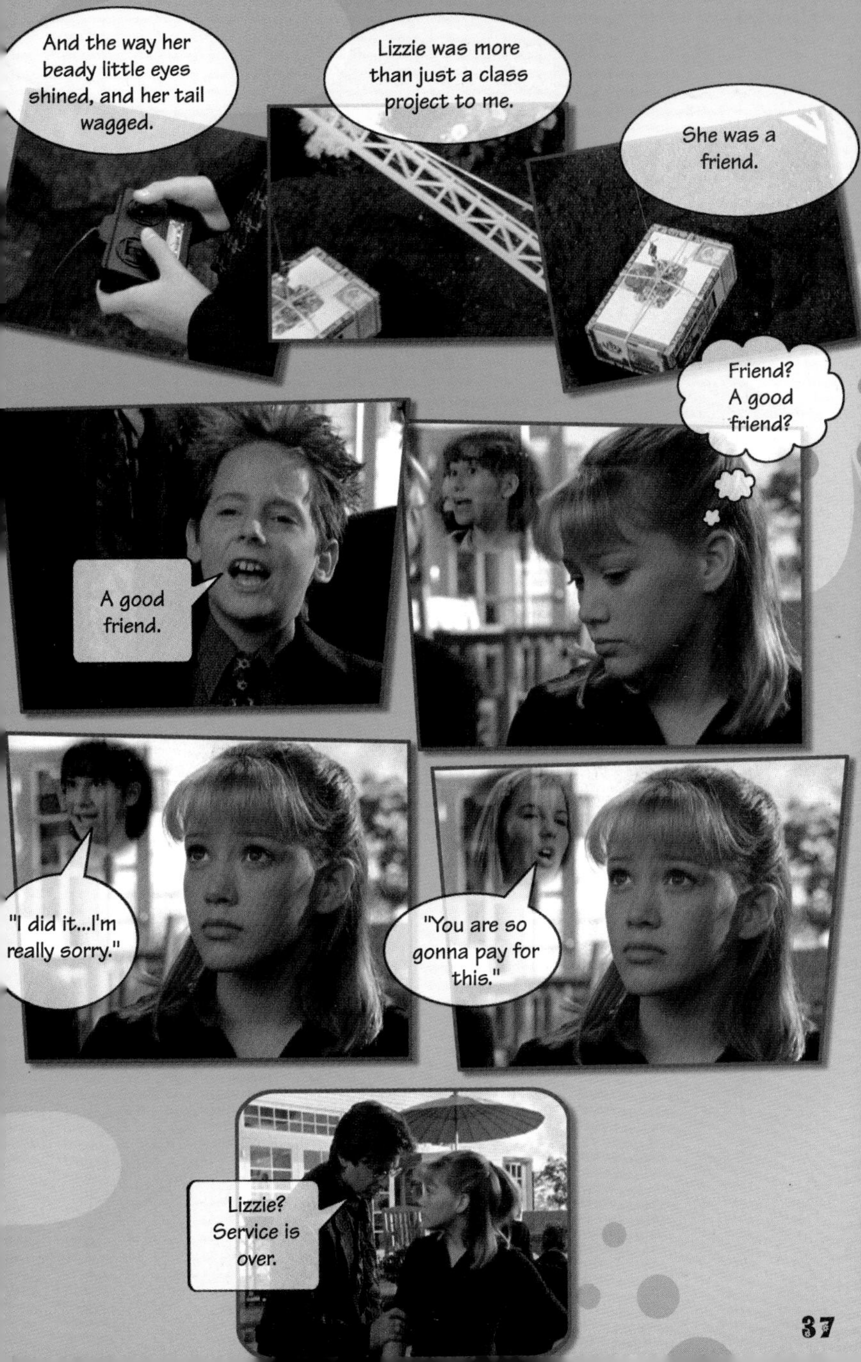

And the way her beady little eyes shined, and her tail wagged.
Lizzie was more than just a class project to me.
She was a friend.
A good friend.
Friend? A good friend?
"I did it...I'm really sorry."
"You are so gonna pay for this."
Lizzie? Service is over.

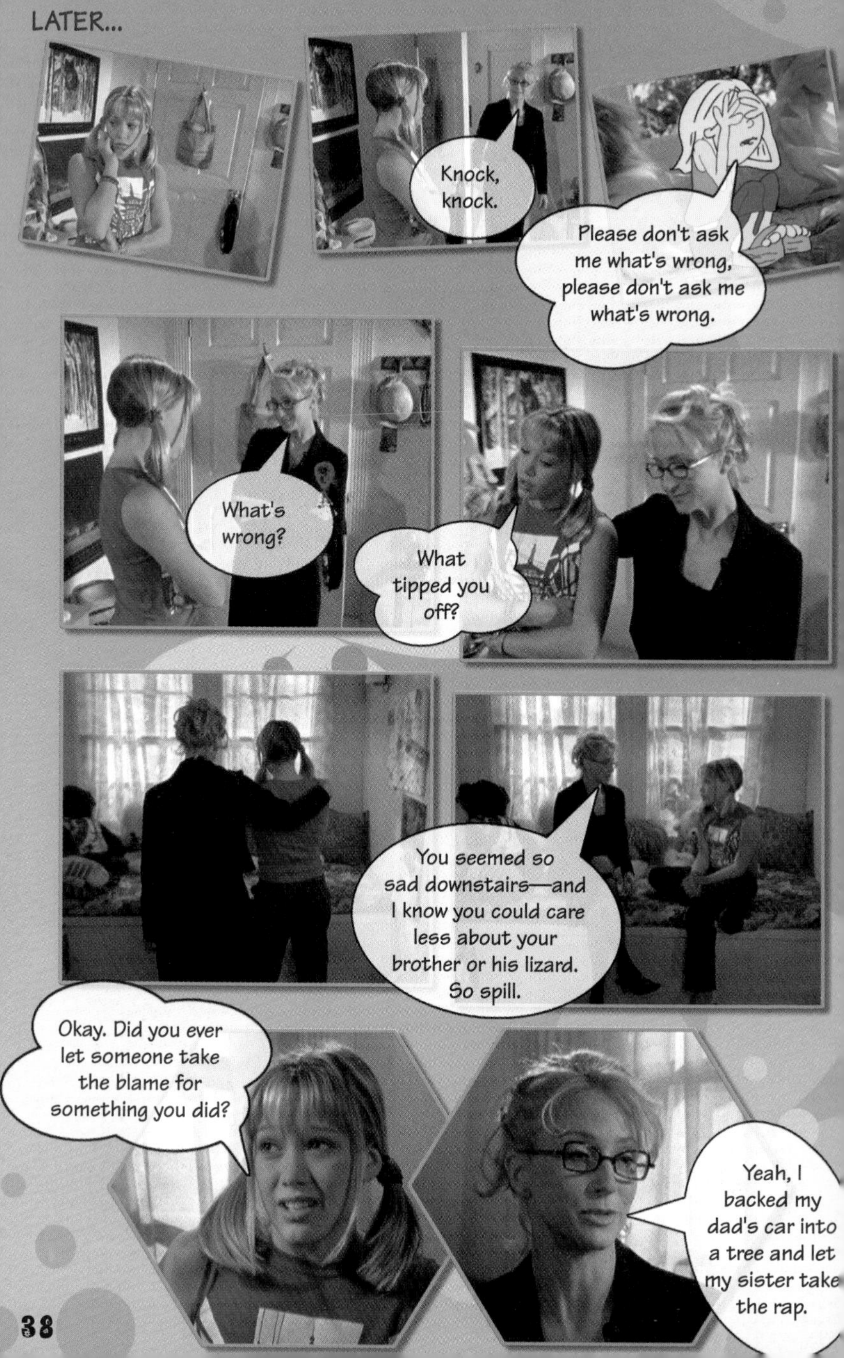
LATER...
Knock, knock.
Please don't ask me what's wrong, please don't ask me what's wrong.
What's wrong?
What tipped you off?
You seemed so sad downstairs—and I know you could care less about your brother or his lizard. So spill.
Okay. Did you ever let someone take the blame for something you did?
Yeah, I backed my dad's car into a tree and let my sister take the rap.

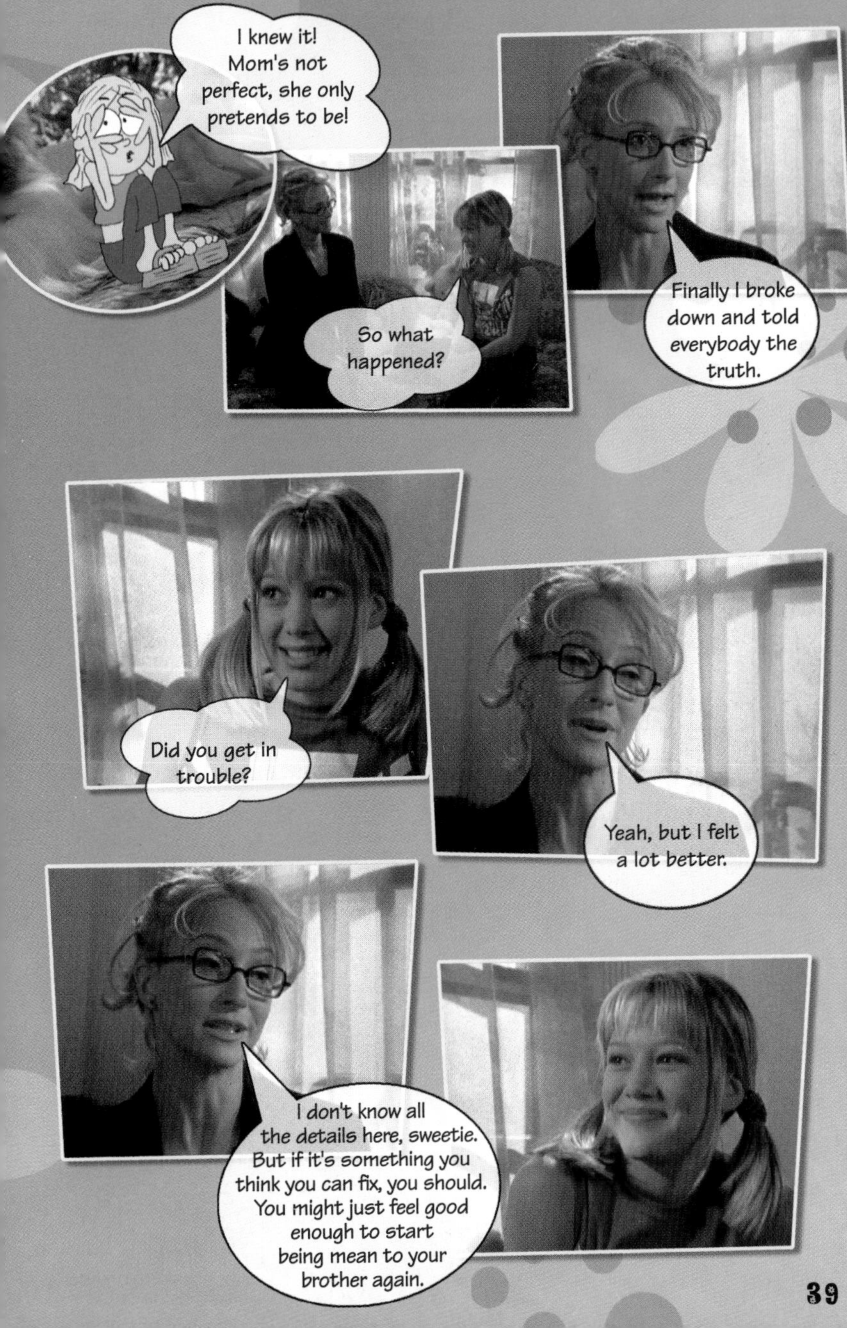
I knew it! Mom's not perfect, she only pretends to be!
So what happened?
Finally I broke down and told everybody the truth.
Did you get in trouble?
Yeah, but I felt a lot better.
I don't know all the details here, sweetie. But if it's something you think you can fix, you should. You might just feel good enough to start being mean to your brother again.

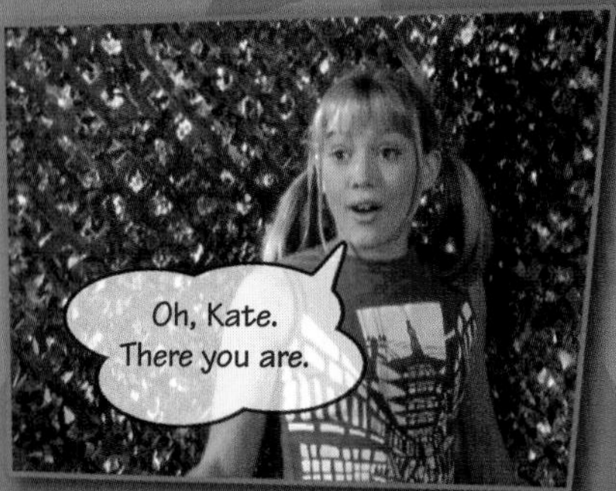
Oh, Kate. There you are.

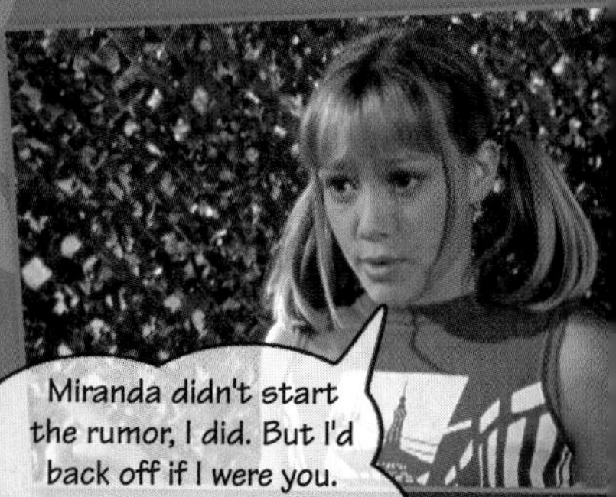
Miranda didn't start the rumor, I did. But I'd back off if I were you. Unless, of course, you want things to get ugly.

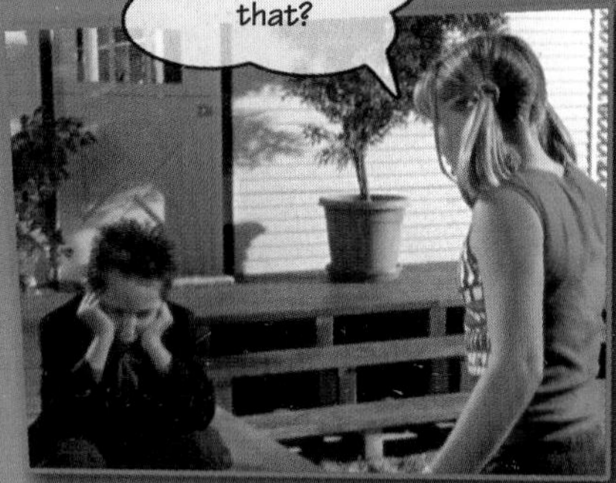
How was that?

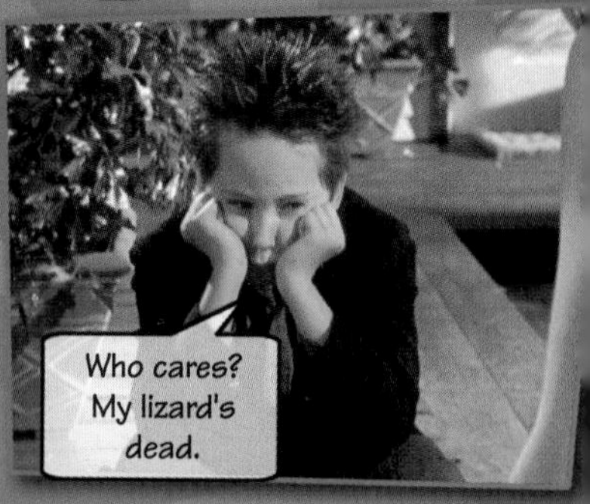
Who cares? My lizard's dead.

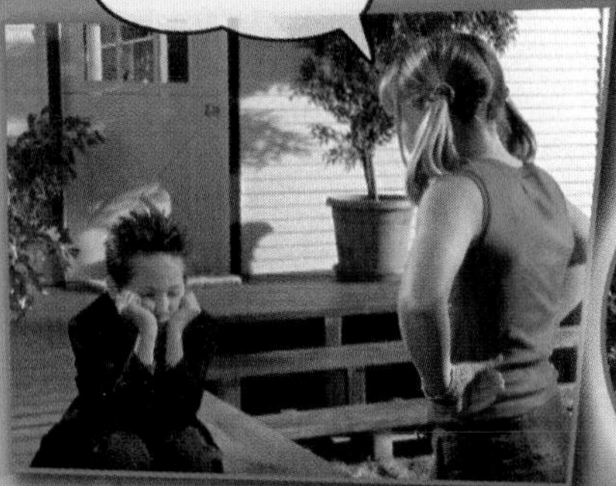
Matt! Pay attention!

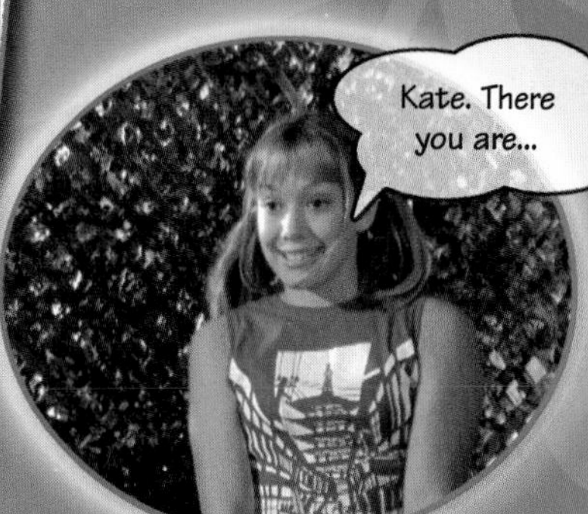
Kate. There you are...

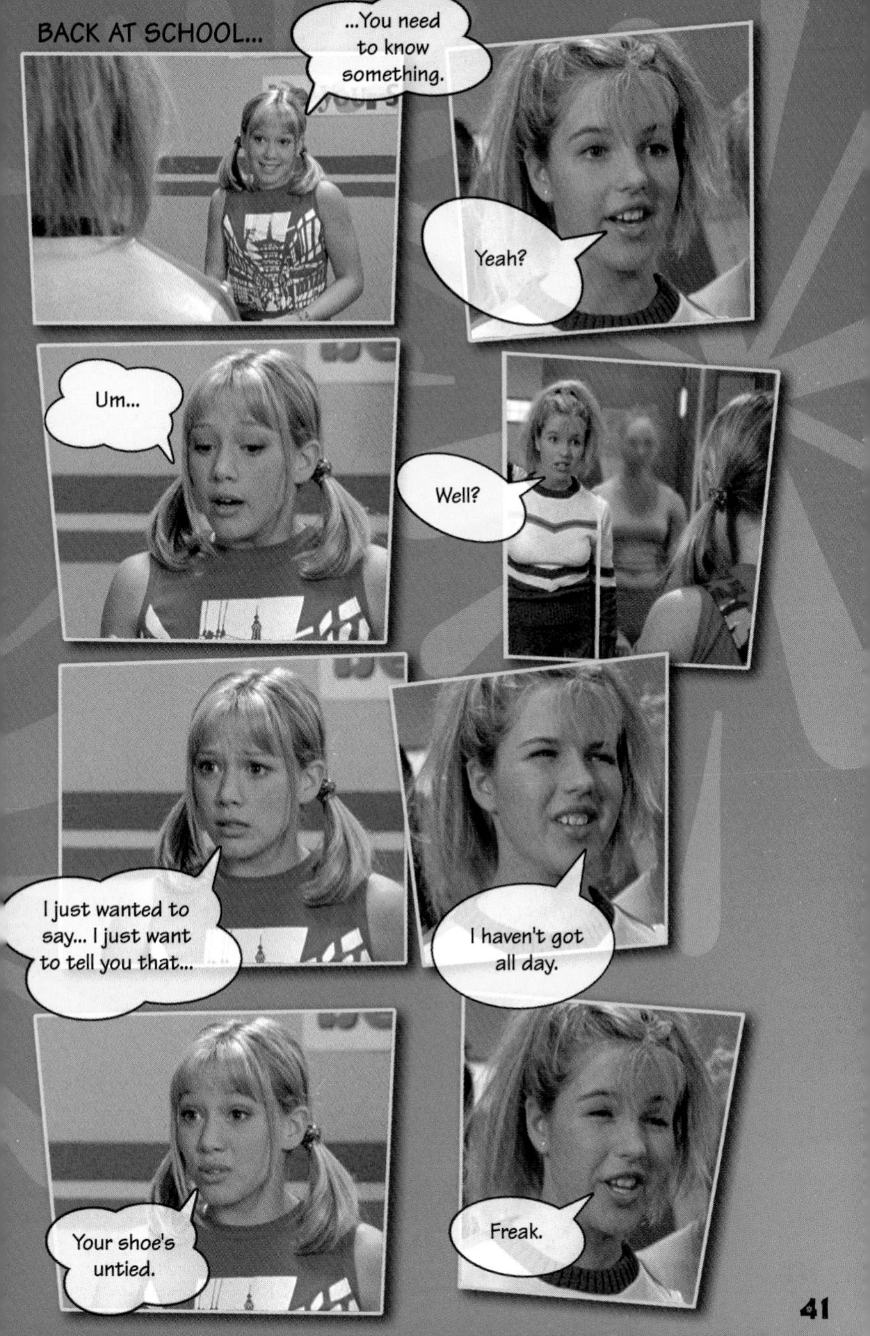
BACK AT SCHOOL...
...You need to know something.
Yeah?
Um...
Well?
I just wanted to say... I just want to tell you that...
I haven't got all day.
Your shoe's untied.
Freak.

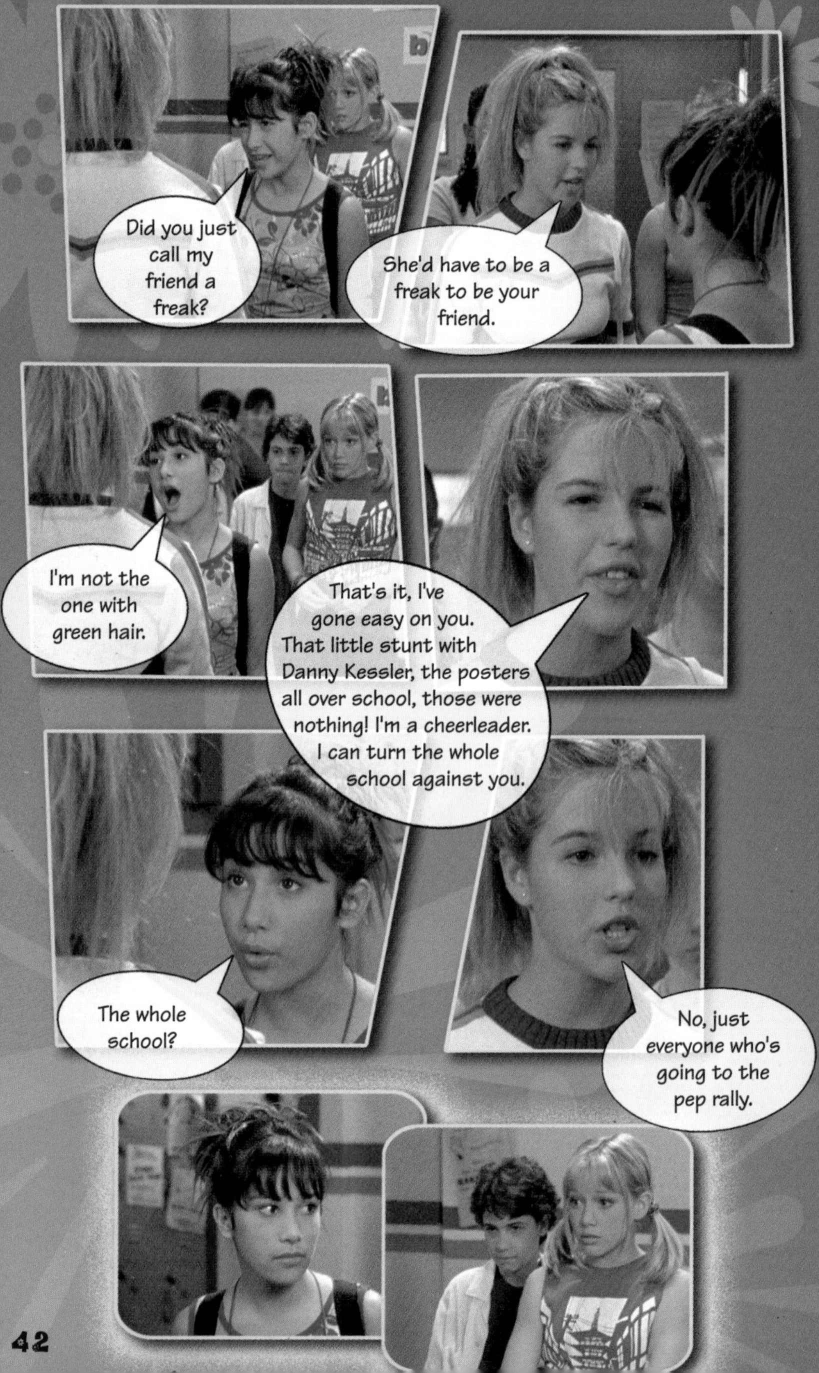
Did you just call my friend a freak?
She'd have to be a freak to be your friend.
I'm not the one with green hair.
That's it, I've gone easy on you. That little stunt with Danny Kessler, the posters all over school, those were nothing! I'm a cheerleader. I can turn the whole school against you.
The whole school?
No, just everyone who's going to the pep rally.

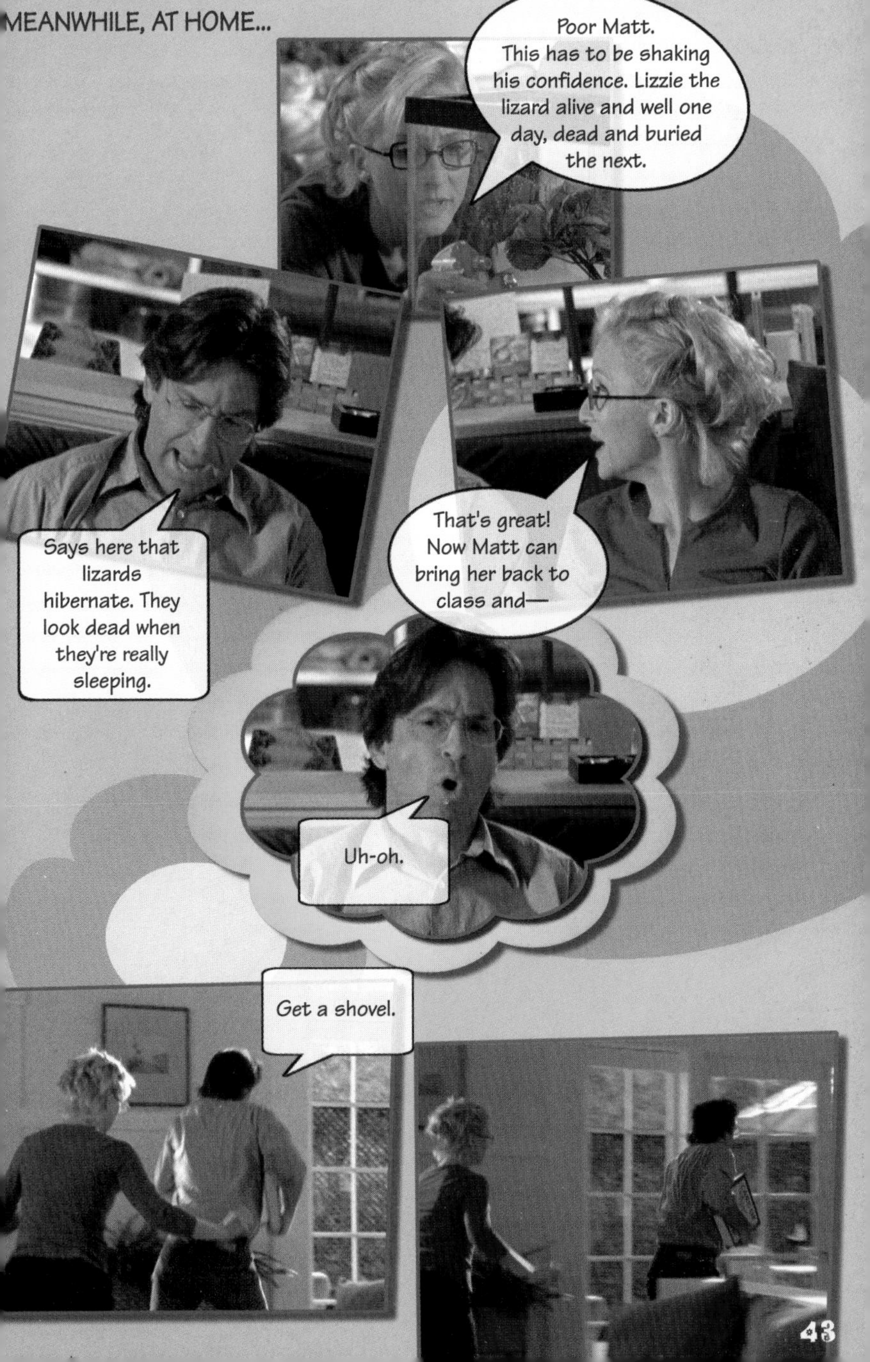
MEANWHILE, AT HOME...
Poor Matt. This has to be shaking his confidence. Lizzie the lizard alive and well one day, dead and buried the next.
Says here that lizards hibernate. They look dead when they're really sleeping.
That's great! Now Matt can bring her back to class and—
Uh-oh.
Get a shovel.

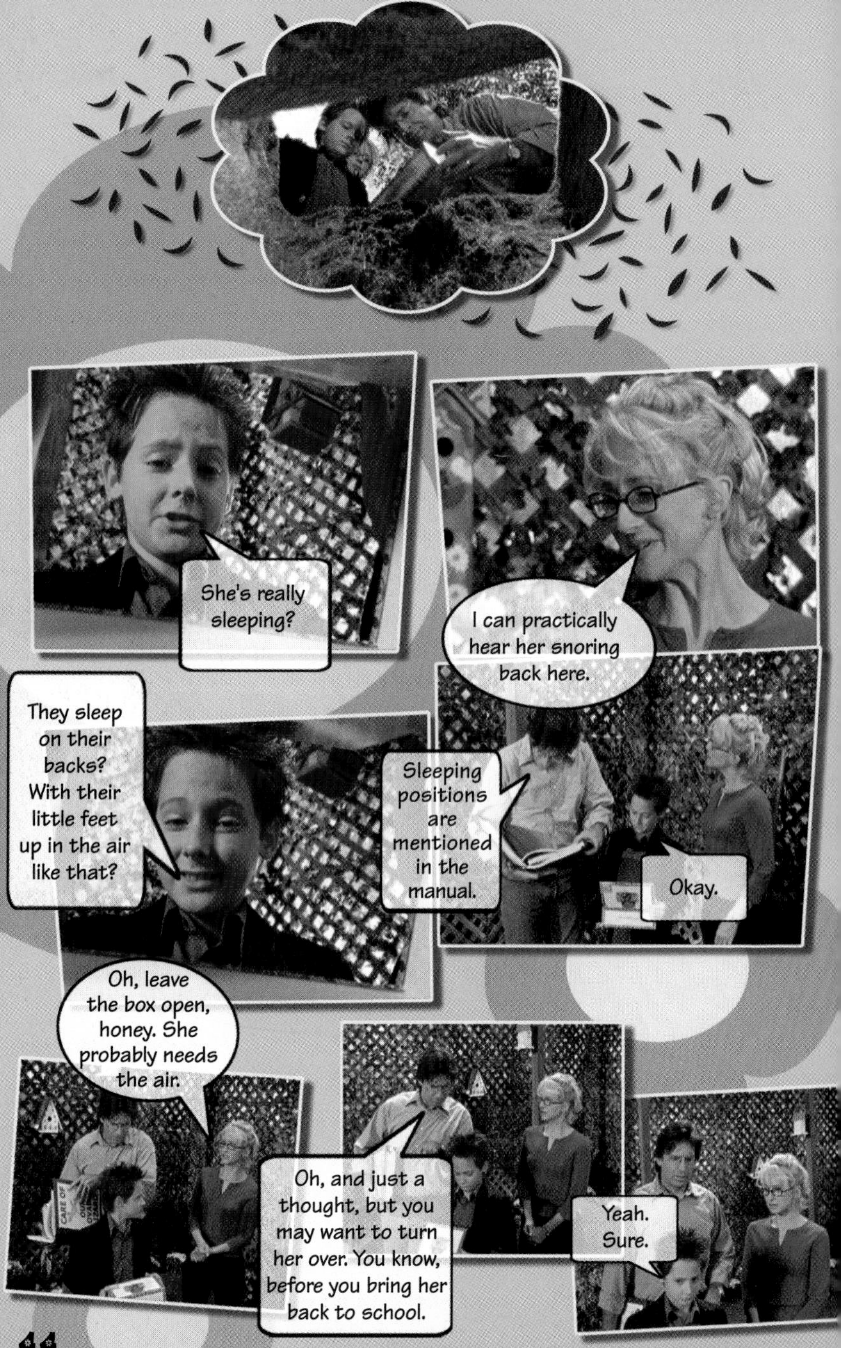

She's really sleeping?
I can practically hear her snoring back here.
They sleep on their backs? With their little feet up in the air like that?
Sleeping positions are mentioned in the manual.
Okay.
Oh, leave the box open, honey. She probably needs the air.
Oh, and just a thought, but you may want to turn her over. You know, before you bring her back to school.
Yeah. Sure.

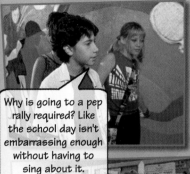

Why is going to a pep rally required? Like the school day isn't embarrassing enough without having to sing about it.

I actually feel kind of sorry for her.

Really?

No.

All right, enough. I'm telling her.

Lizzie, don't! I can handle this.

Well, so can I. I think.

No, I know I can. I started this thing and now I'm finally going to take responsibility for it.

45

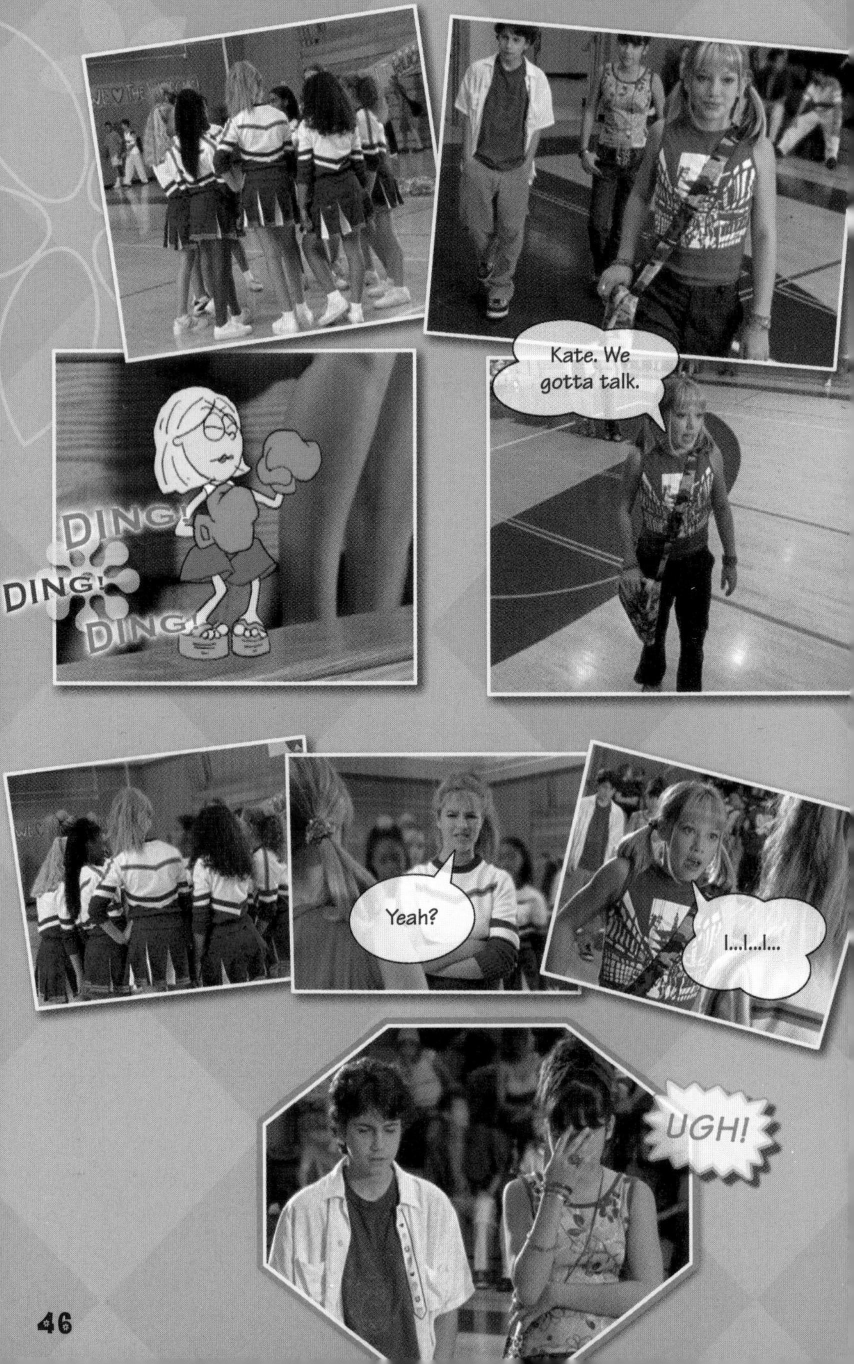
Kate. We gotta talk.
DING!
DING!
DING!
Yeah?
I...I...I...
UGH!

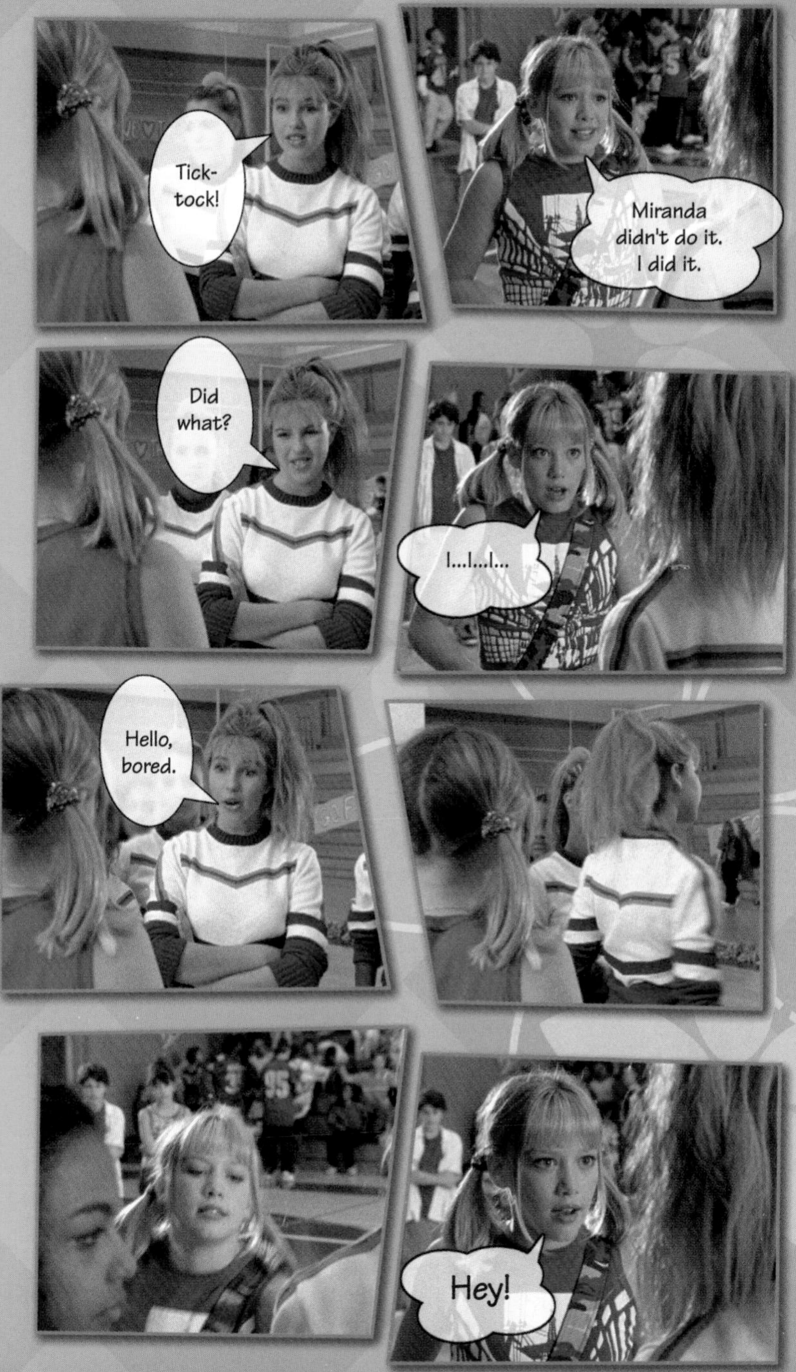
Tick-tock!
Miranda didn't do it. I did it.
Did what?
I...I...I...
Hello, bored.
Hey!

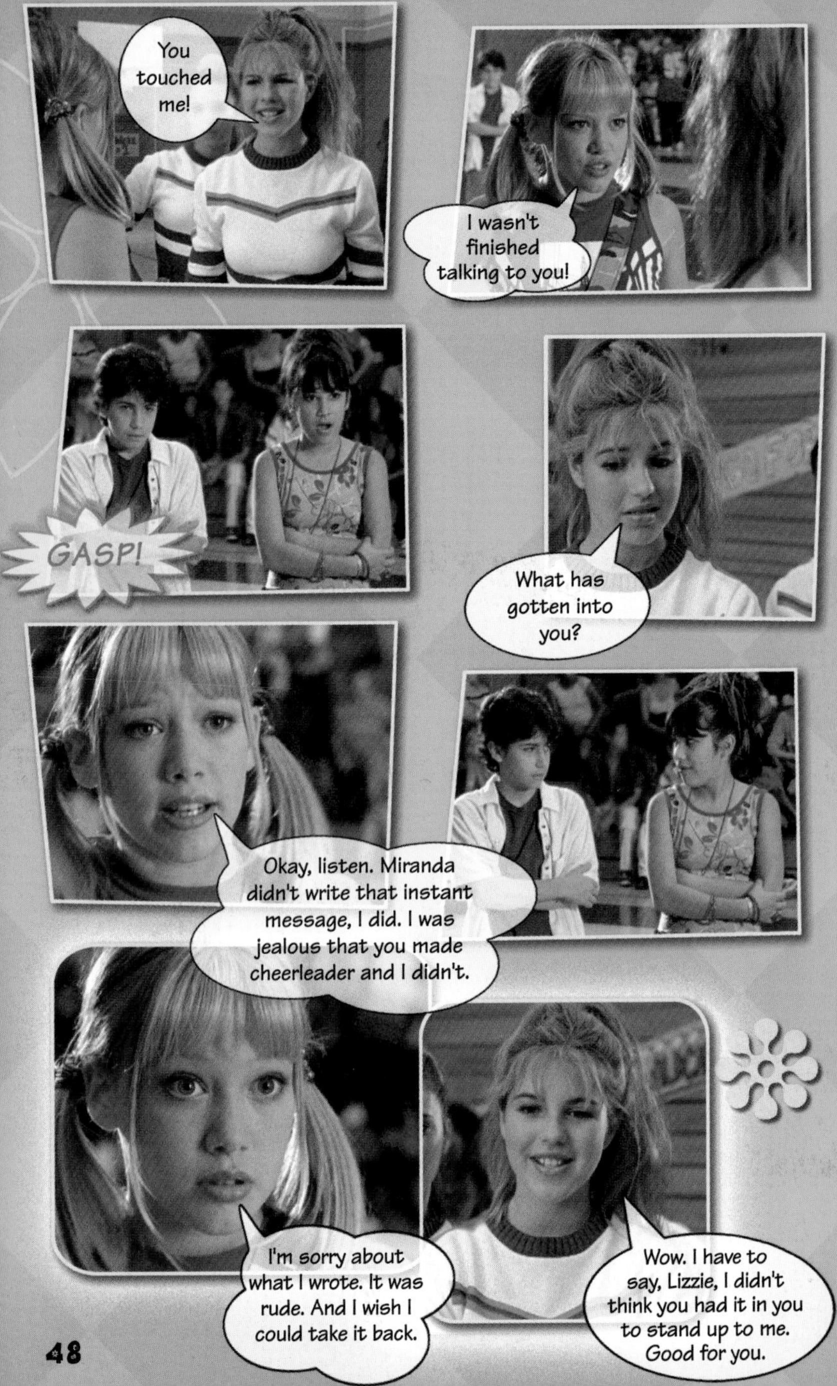

You touched me!
I wasn't finished talking to you!
GASP!
What has gotten into you?
Okay, listen. Miranda didn't write that instant message, I did. I was jealous that you made cheerleader and I didn't.
I'm sorry about what I wrote. It was rude. And I wish I could take it back.
Wow. I have to say, Lizzie, I didn't think you had it in you to stand up to me. Good for you.

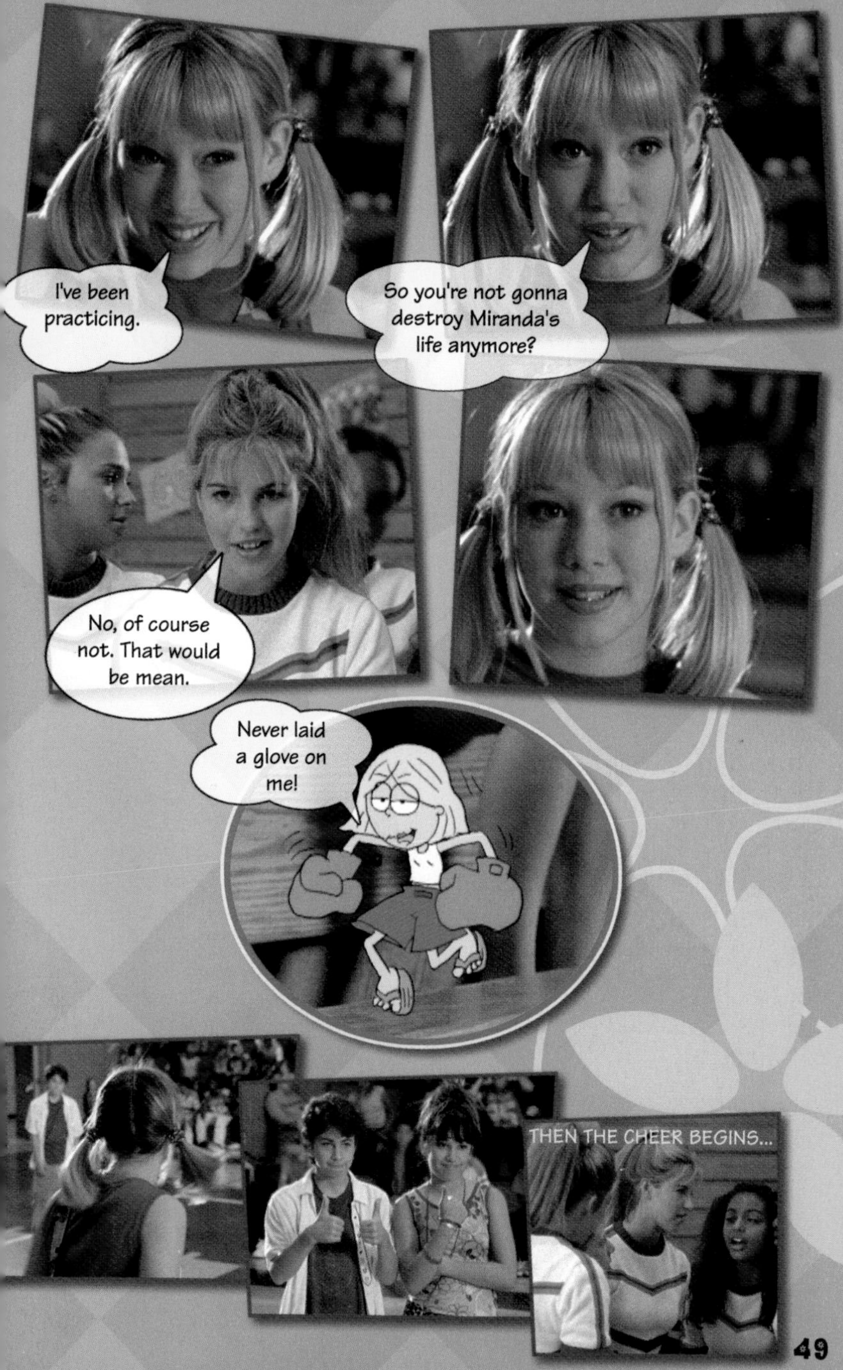
I've been practicing.
So you're not gonna destroy Miranda's life anymore?
No, of course not. That would be mean.
Never laid a glove on me!
THEN THE CHEER BEGINS...

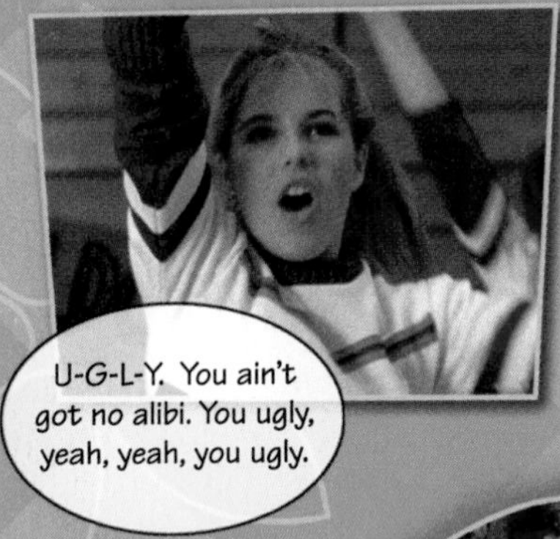
U-G-L-Y. You ain't got no alibi. You ugly, yeah, yeah, you ugly.

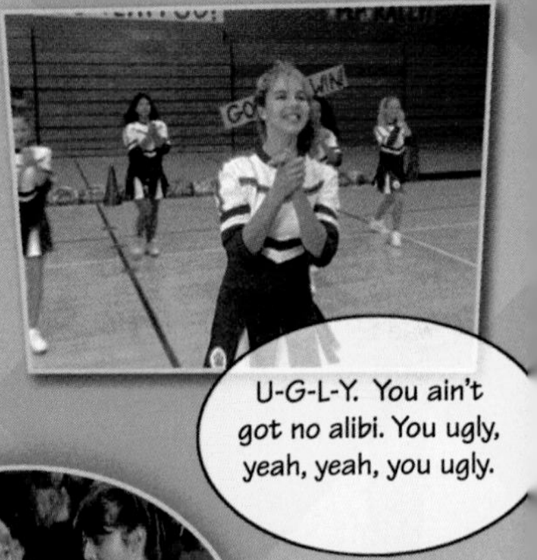
U-G-L-Y. You ain't got no alibi. You ugly, yeah, yeah, you ugly.

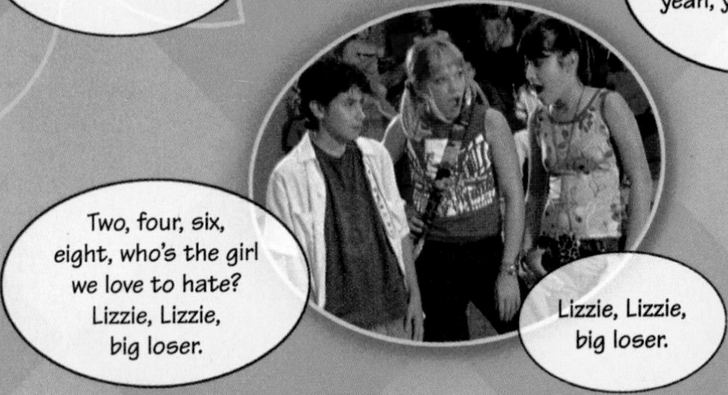
Two, four, six, eight, who's the girl we love to hate? Lizzie, Lizzie, big loser.
Lizzie, Lizzie, big loser.

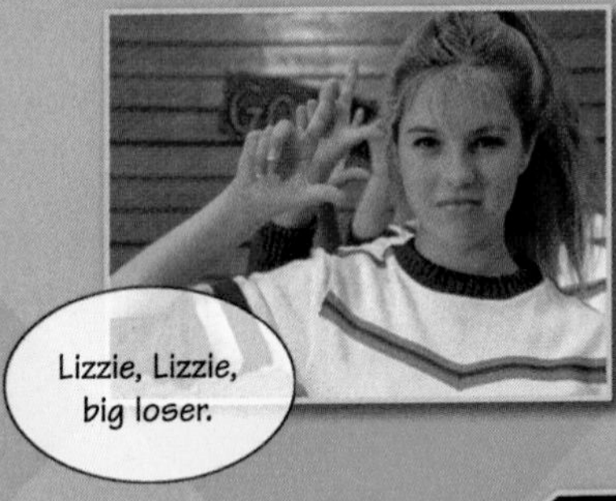
Lizzie, Lizzie, big loser.

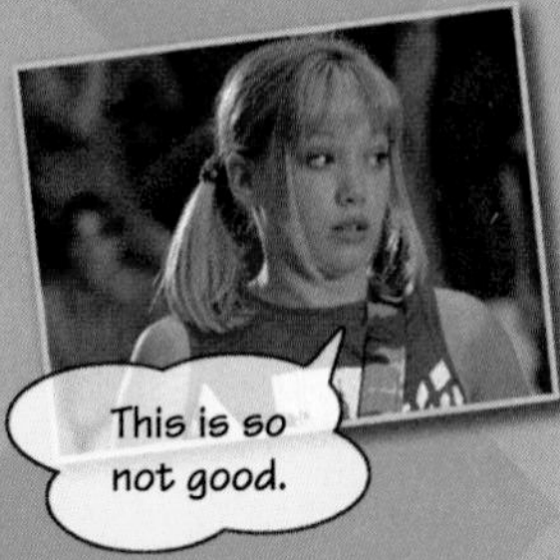
This is so not good.

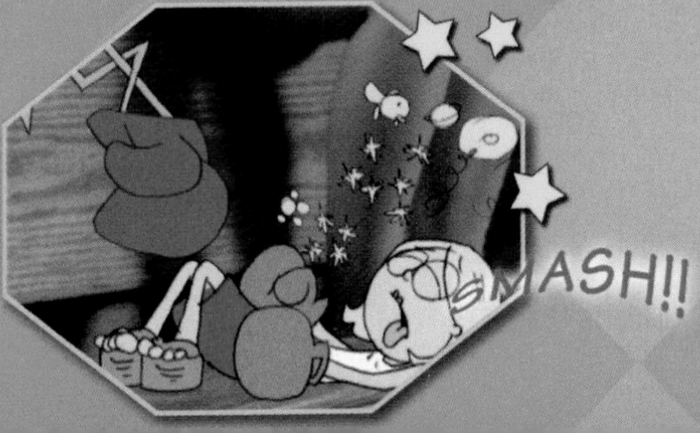
SMASH!!

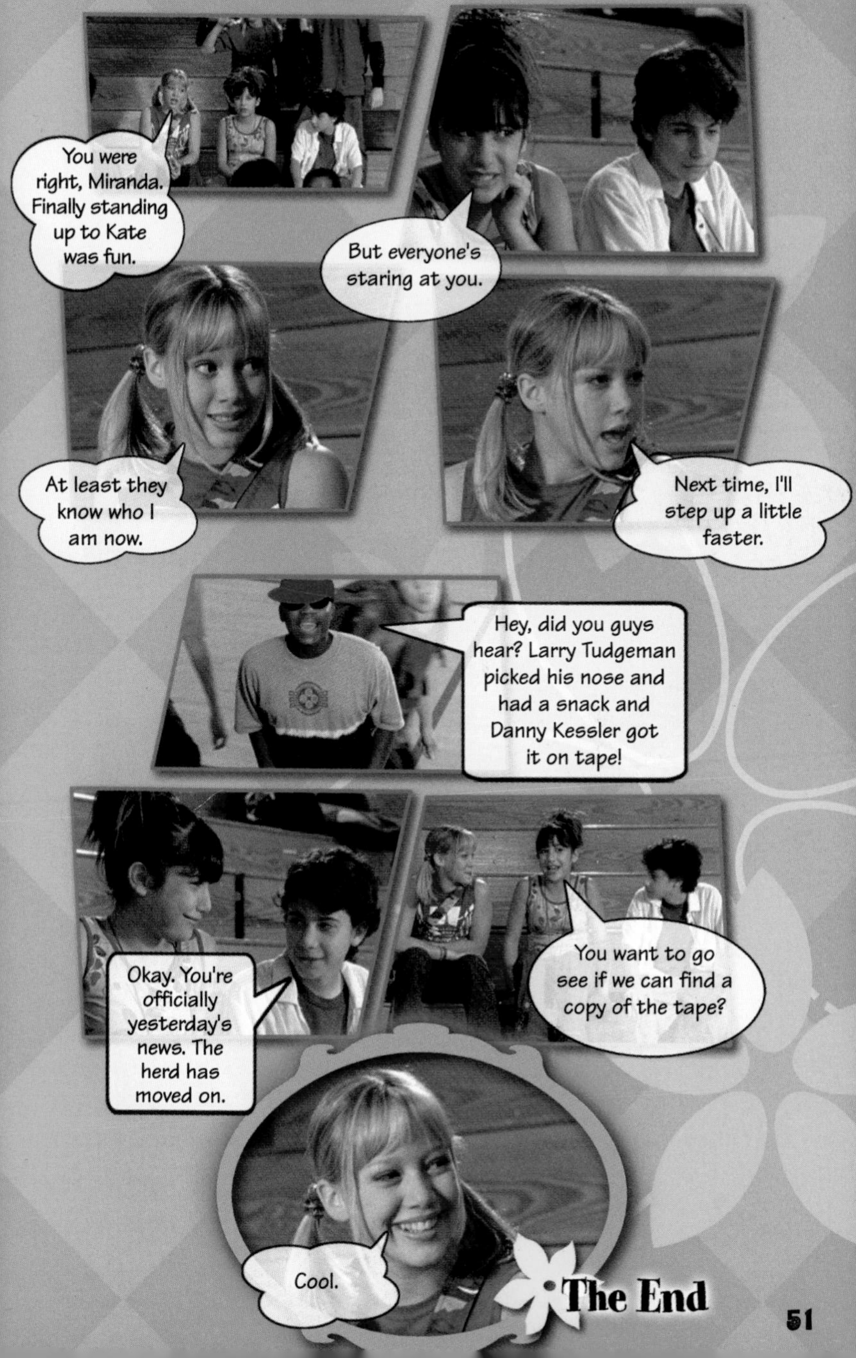
You were right, Miranda. Finally standing up to Kate was fun.
But everyone's staring at you.
At least they know who I am now.
Next time, I'll step up a little faster.
Hey, did you guys hear? Larry Tudgeman picked his nose and had a snack and Danny Kessler got it on tape!
Okay. You're officially yesterday's news. The herd has moved on.
You want to go see if we can find a copy of the tape?
Cool.
The End

Lizzie McGuire

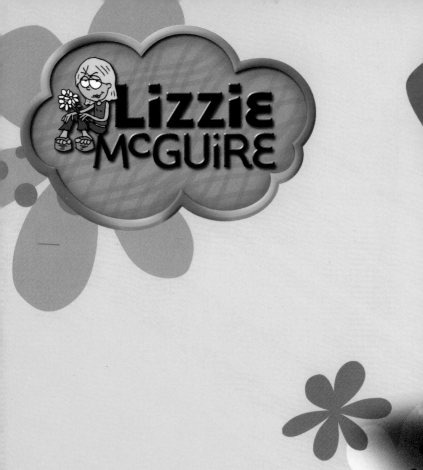

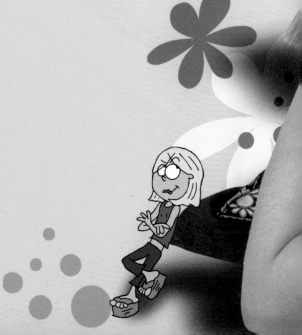

Episode 4

"Jack of All Trades"

A test at school leaves Lizzie, Miranda and Gordo thinking about their futures. Meanwhile, Matt tries on a new image and even a new name. It takes a bit of figuring out, but Lizzie and her friends discover that trying on ideas that don't fit exactly right is the only way to find the ones that do.

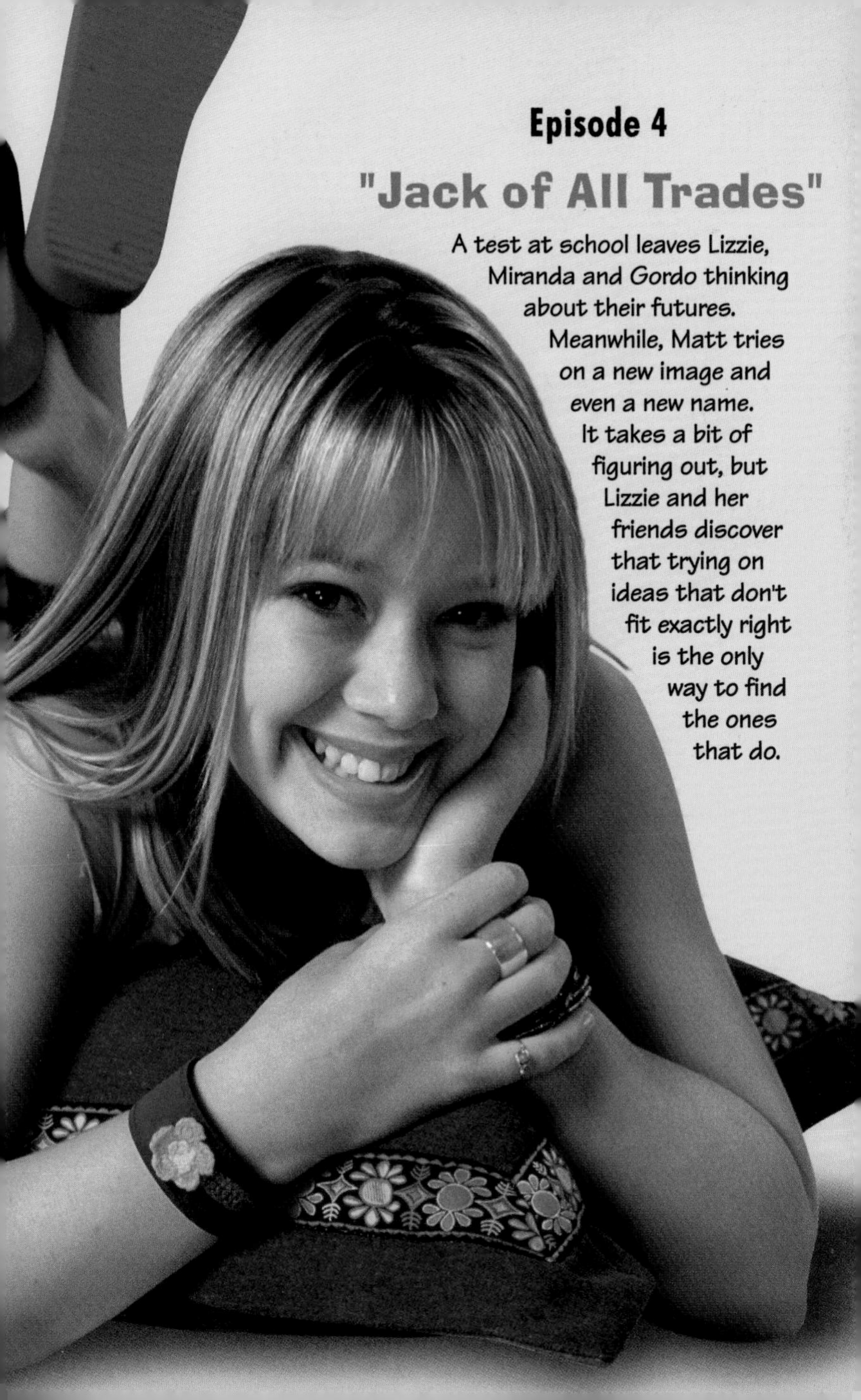

AT SCHOOL...

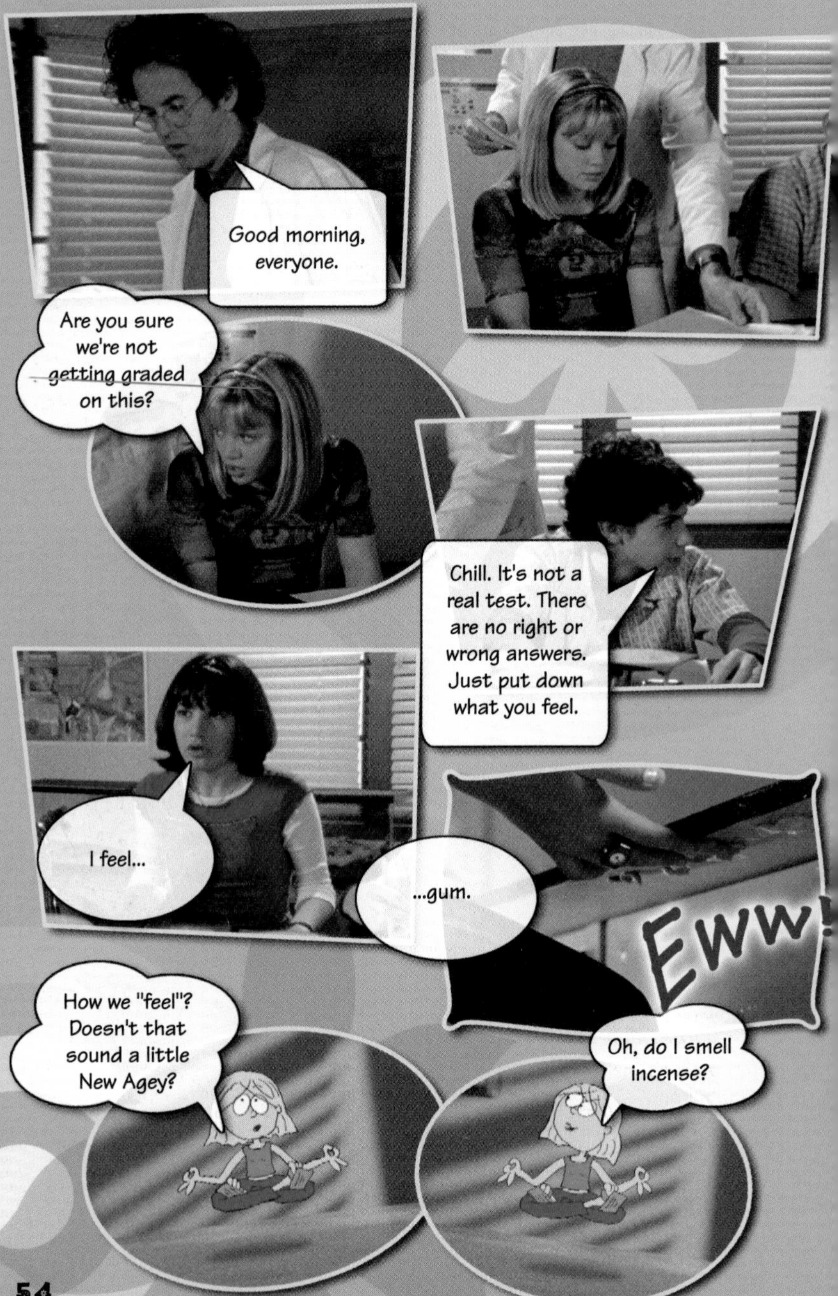
Good morning, everyone.
Are you sure we're not getting graded on this?
Chill. It's not a real test. There are no right or wrong answers. Just put down what you feel.
I feel...
...gum.
Eww!
How we "feel"? Doesn't that sound a little New Agey?
Oh, do I smell incense?

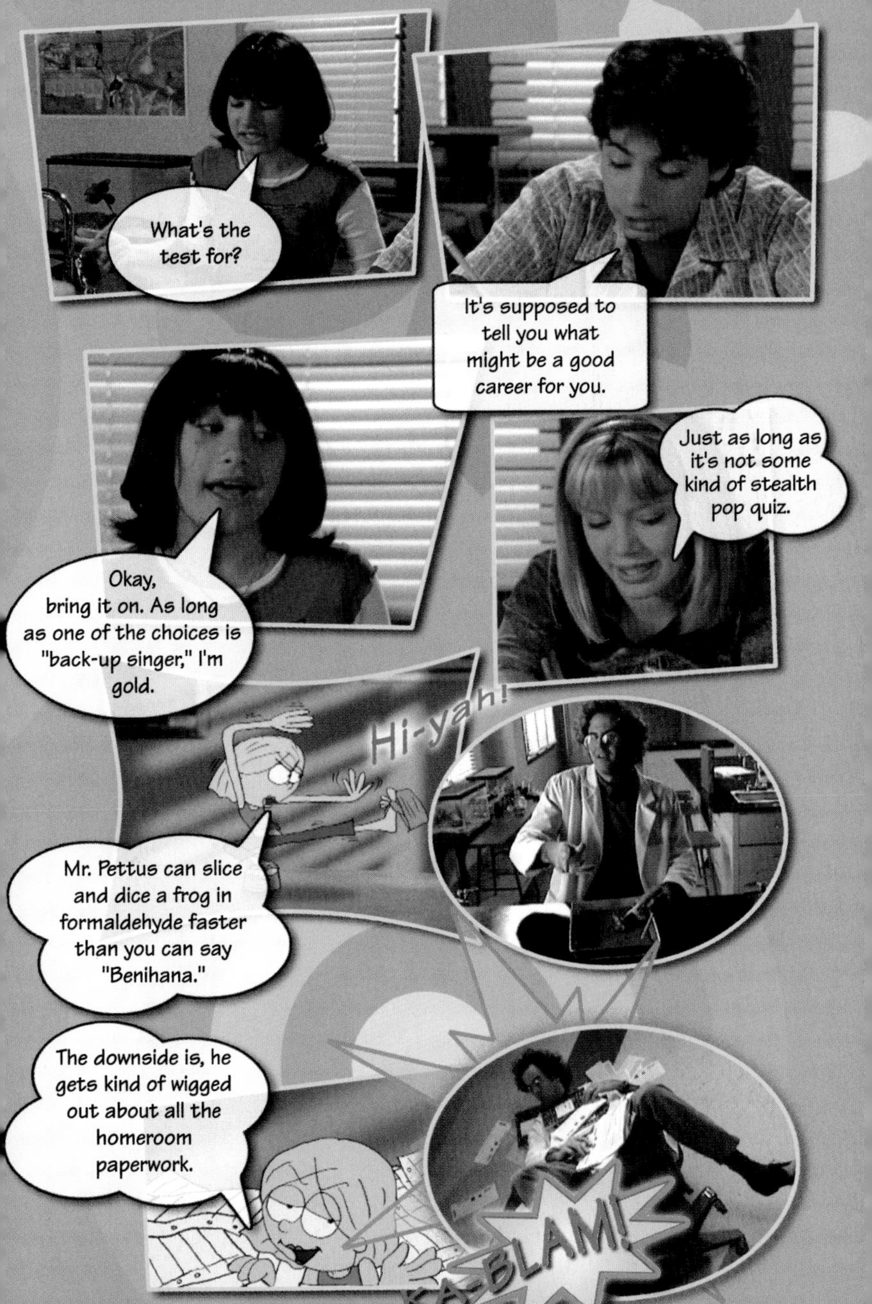
What's the test for?
It's supposed to tell you what might be a good career for you.
Okay, bring it on. As long as one of the choices is "back-up singer," I'm gold.
Just as long as it's not some kind of stealth pop quiz.
Hi-yah!
Mr. Pettus can slice and dice a frog in formaldehyde faster than you can say "Benihana."
The downside is, he gets kind of wigged out about all the homeroom paperwork.
KA-BLAM!

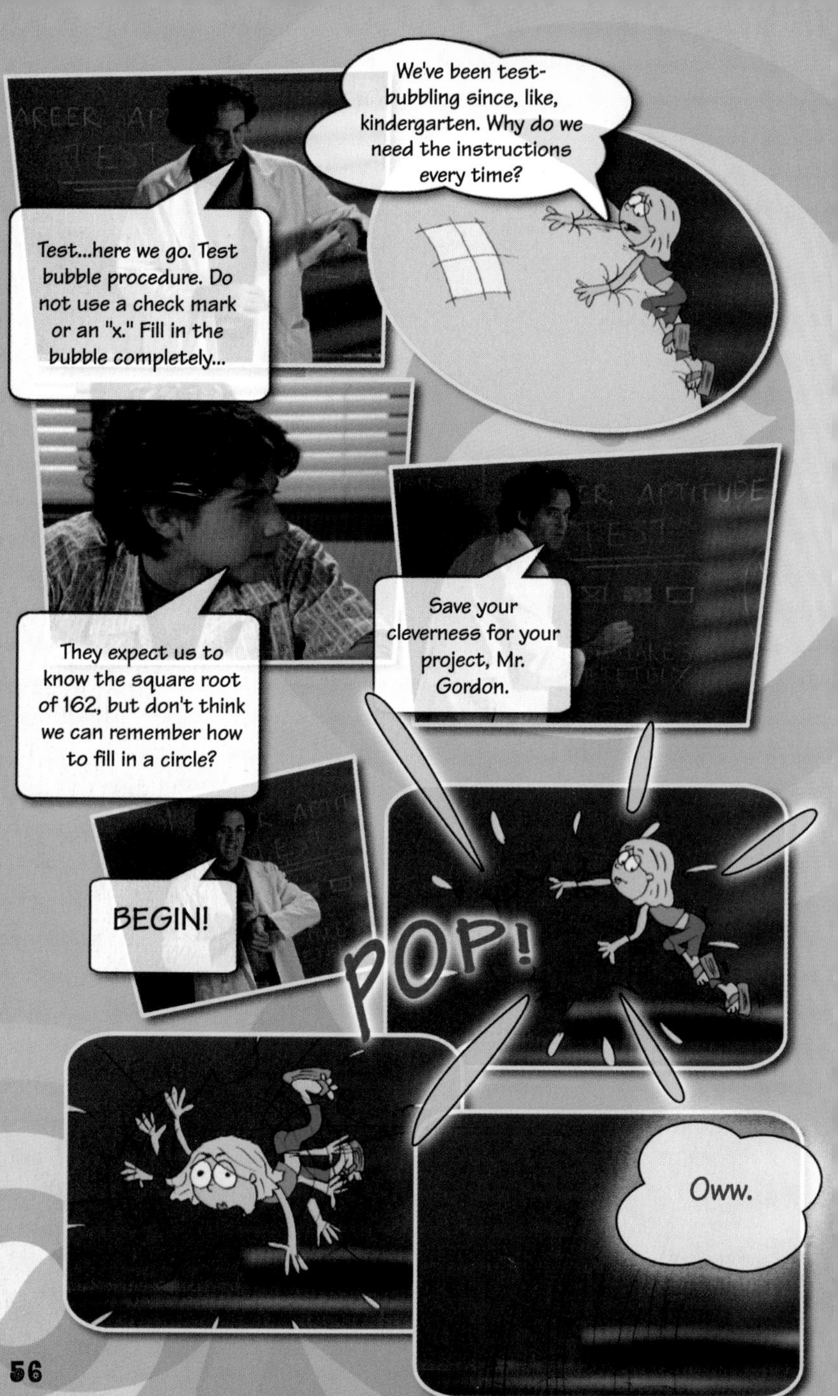

Test...here we go. Test bubble procedure. Do not use a check mark or an "x." Fill in the bubble completely...
We've been test-bubbling since, like, kindergarten. Why do we need the instructions every time?
They expect us to know the square root of 162, but don't think we can remember how to fill in a circle?
Save your cleverness for your project, Mr. Gordon.
BEGIN!
POP!
Oww.

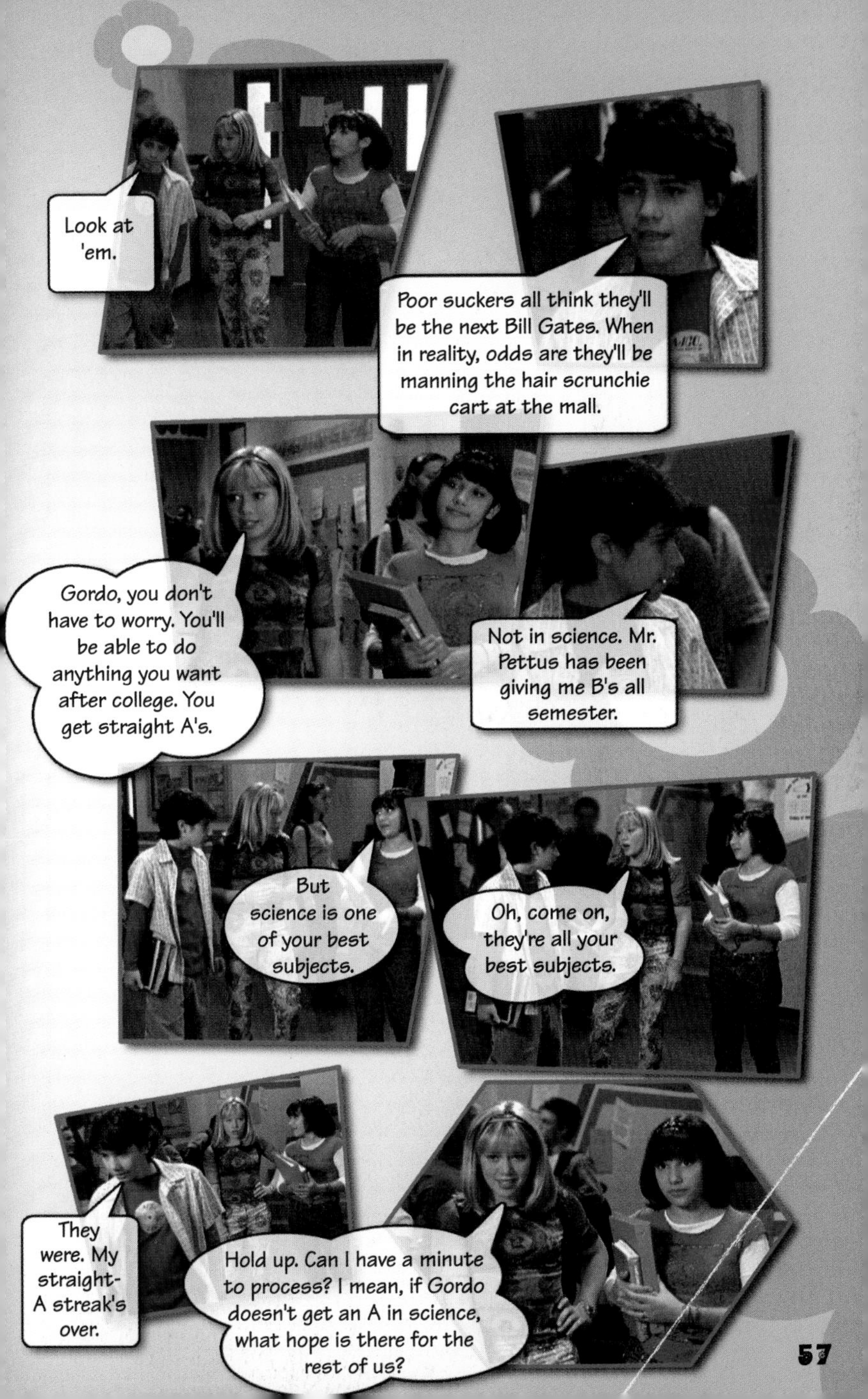
Look at 'em.
Poor suckers all think they'll be the next Bill Gates. When in reality, odds are they'll be manning the hair scrunchie cart at the mall.
Gordo, you don't have to worry. You'll be able to do anything you want after college. You get straight A's.
Not in science. Mr. Pettus has been giving me B's all semester.
But science is one of your best subjects.
Oh, come on, they're all your best subjects.
They were. My straight-A streak's over.
Hold up. Can I have a minute to process? I mean, if Gordo doesn't get an A in science, what hope is there for the rest of us?

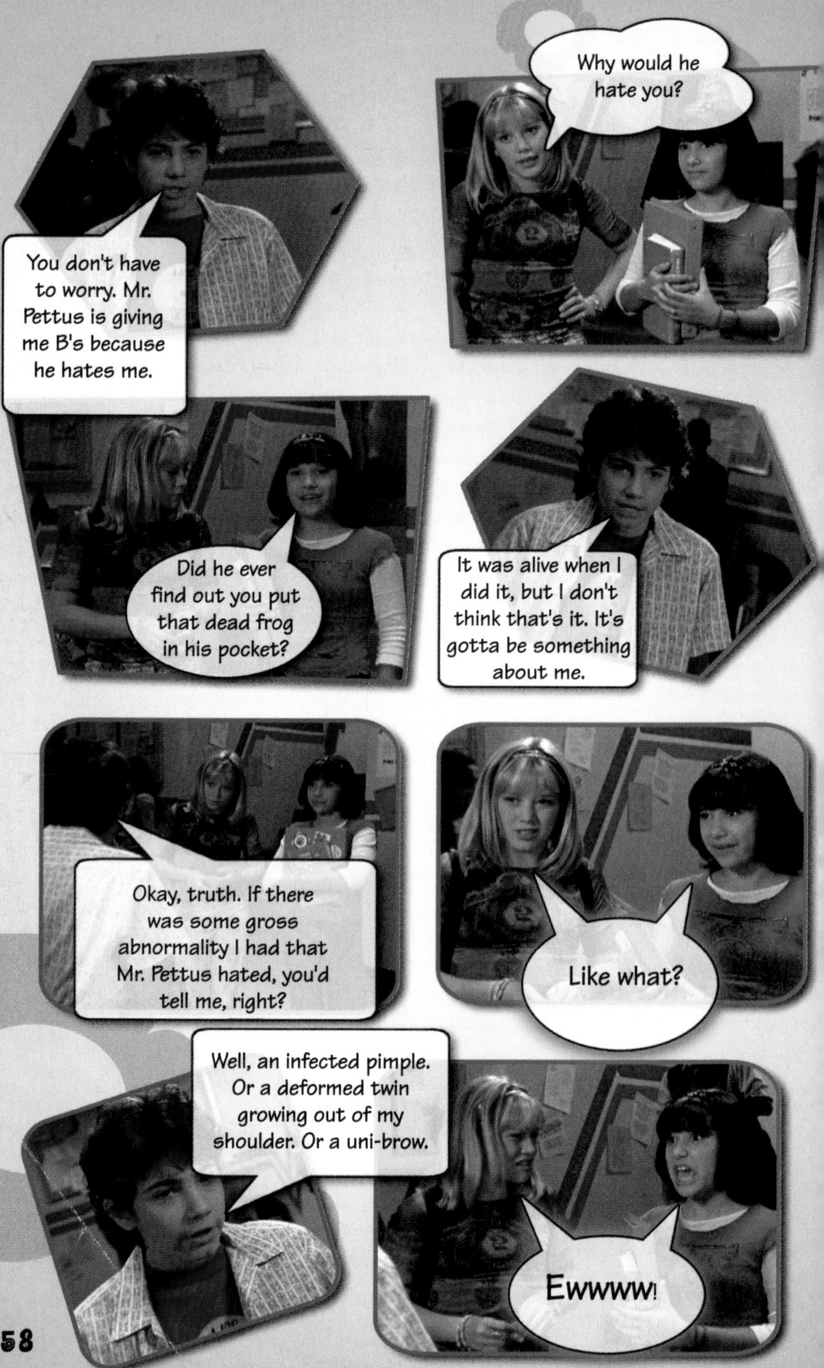
You don't have to worry. Mr. Pettus is giving me B's because he hates me.
Why would he hate you?
Did he ever find out you put that dead frog in his pocket?
It was alive when I did it, but I don't think that's it. It's gotta be something about me.
Okay, truth. If there was some gross abnormality I had that Mr. Pettus hated, you'd tell me, right?
Like what?
Well, an infected pimple. Or a deformed twin growing out of my shoulder. Or a uni-brow.
Ewwww!

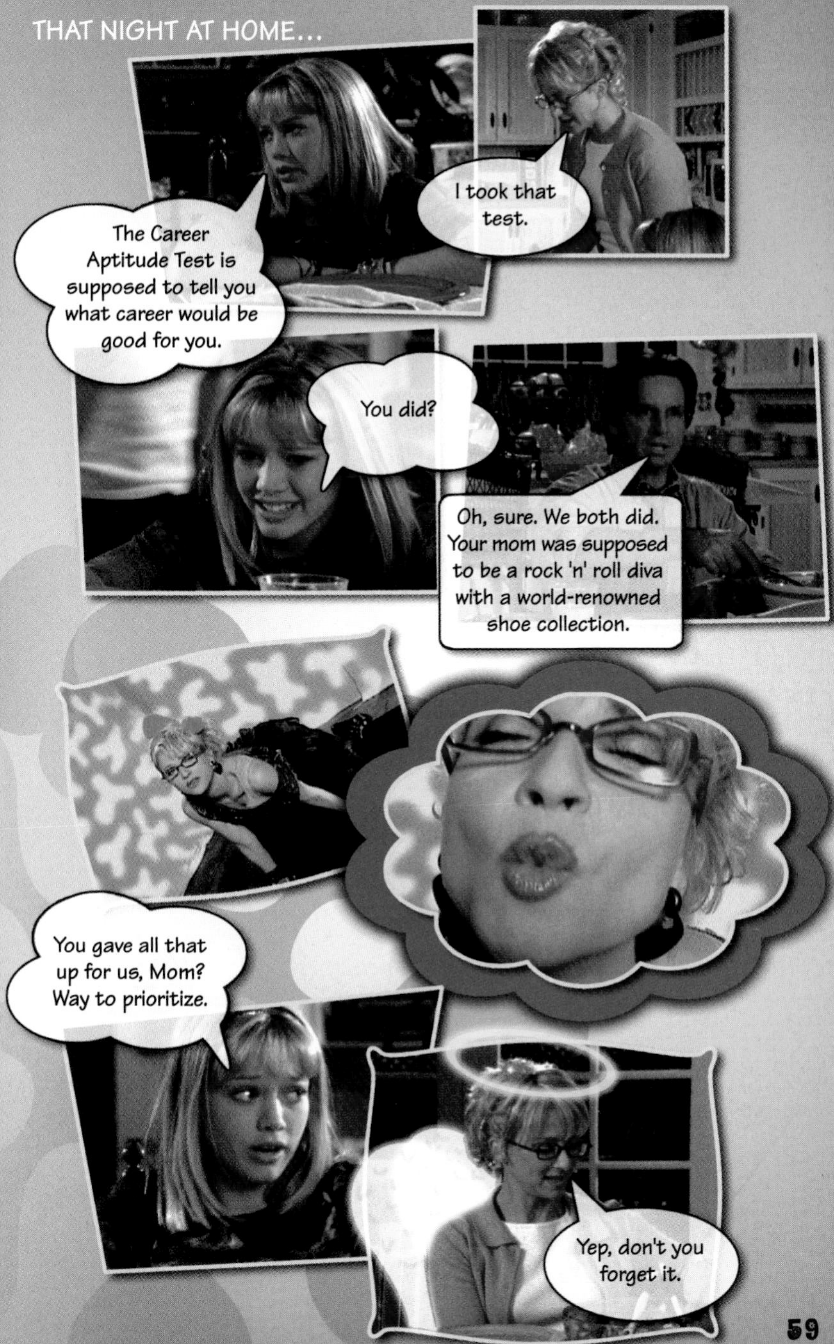
THAT NIGHT AT HOME...
The Career Aptitude Test is supposed to tell you what career would be good for you.
I took that test.
You did?
Oh, sure. We both did. Your mom was supposed to be a rock 'n' roll diva with a world-renowned shoe collection.
You gave all that up for us, Mom? Way to prioritize.
Yep, don't you forget it.

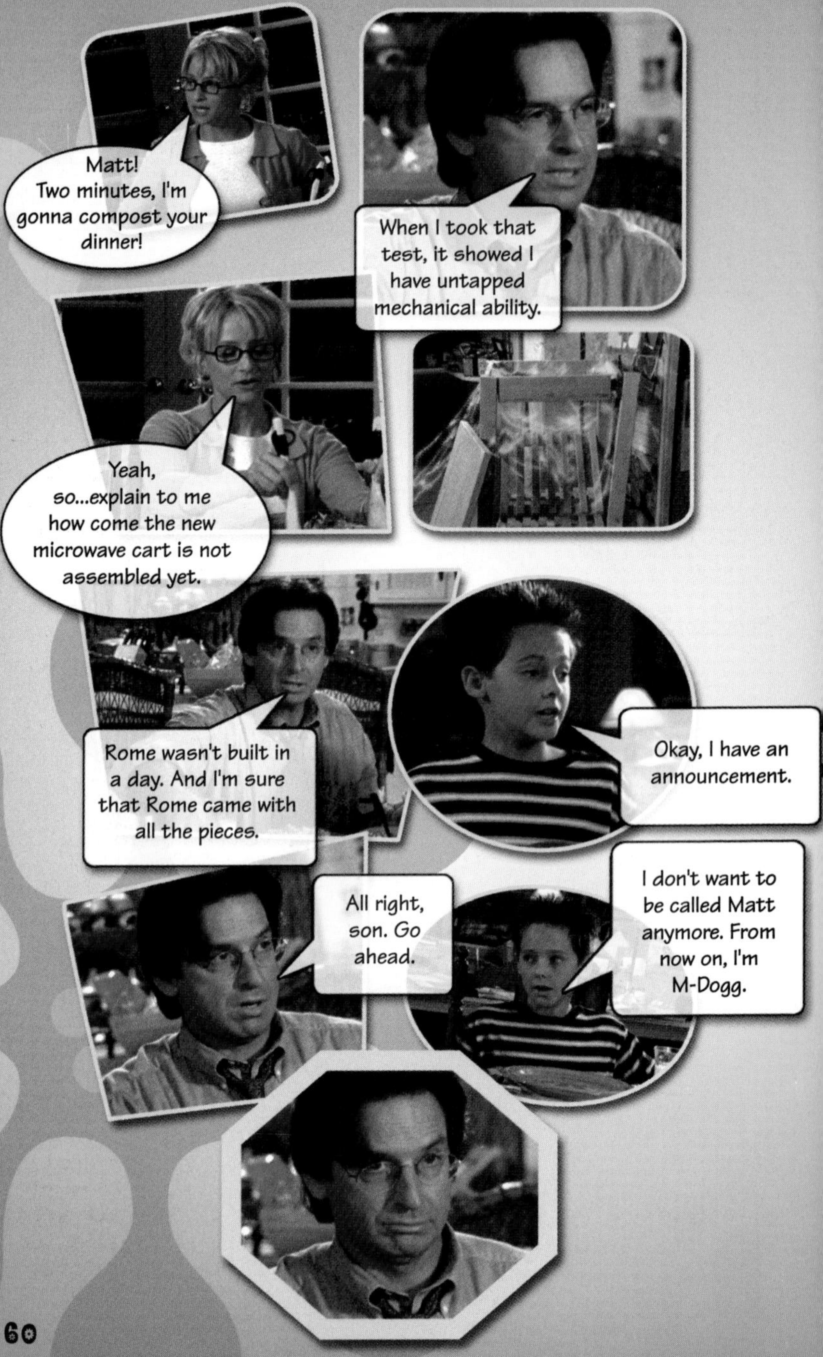
Matt! Two minutes, I'm gonna compost your dinner!
When I took that test, it showed I have untapped mechanical ability.
Yeah, so...explain to me how come the new microwave cart is not assembled yet.
Rome wasn't built in a day. And I'm sure that Rome came with all the pieces.
Okay, I have an announcement.
All right, son. Go ahead.
I don't want to be called Matt anymore. From now on, I'm M-Dogg.

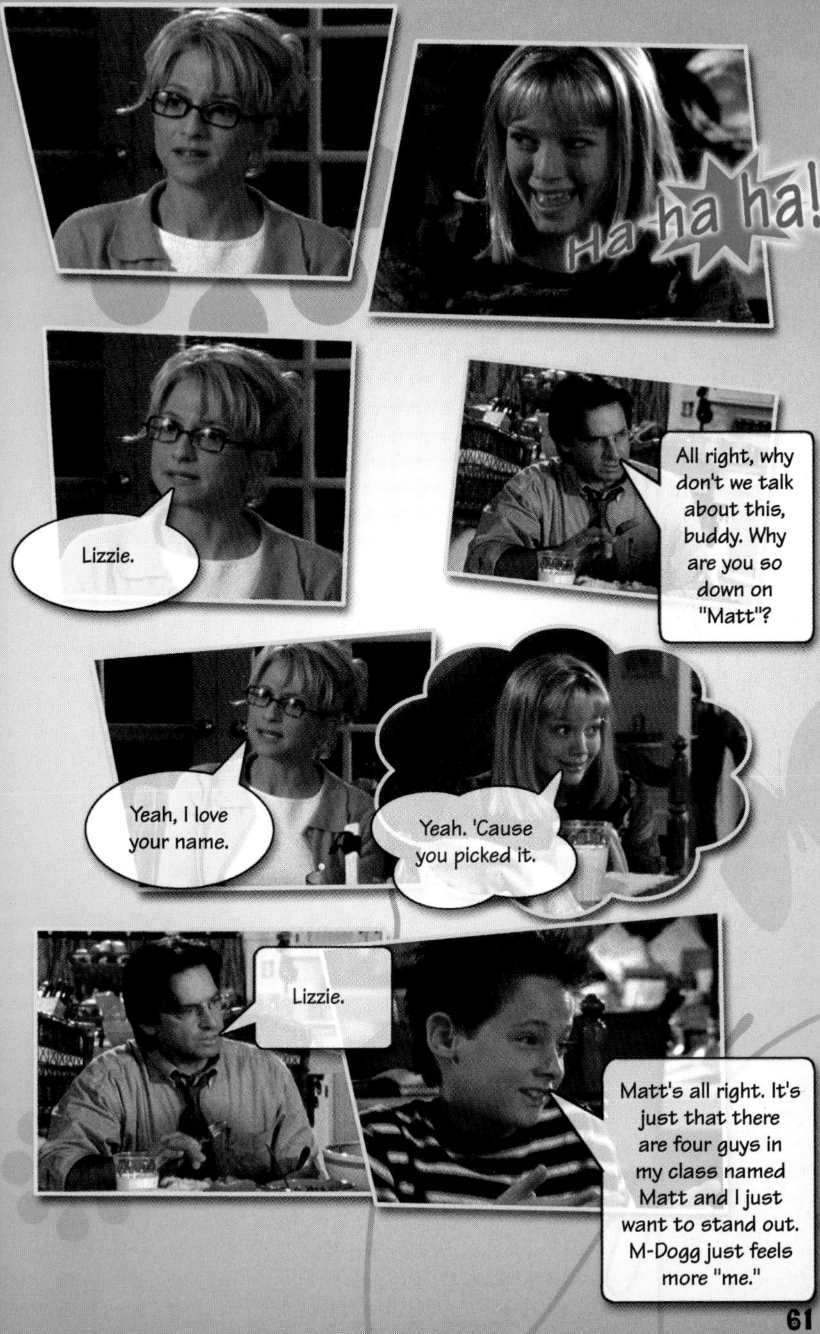
Ha ha ha!
Lizzie.
All right, why don't we talk about this, buddy. Why are you so down on "Matt"?
Yeah, I love your name.
Yeah. 'Cause you picked it.
Lizzie.
Matt's all right. It's just that there are four guys in my class named Matt and I just want to stand out. M-Dogg just feels more "me."

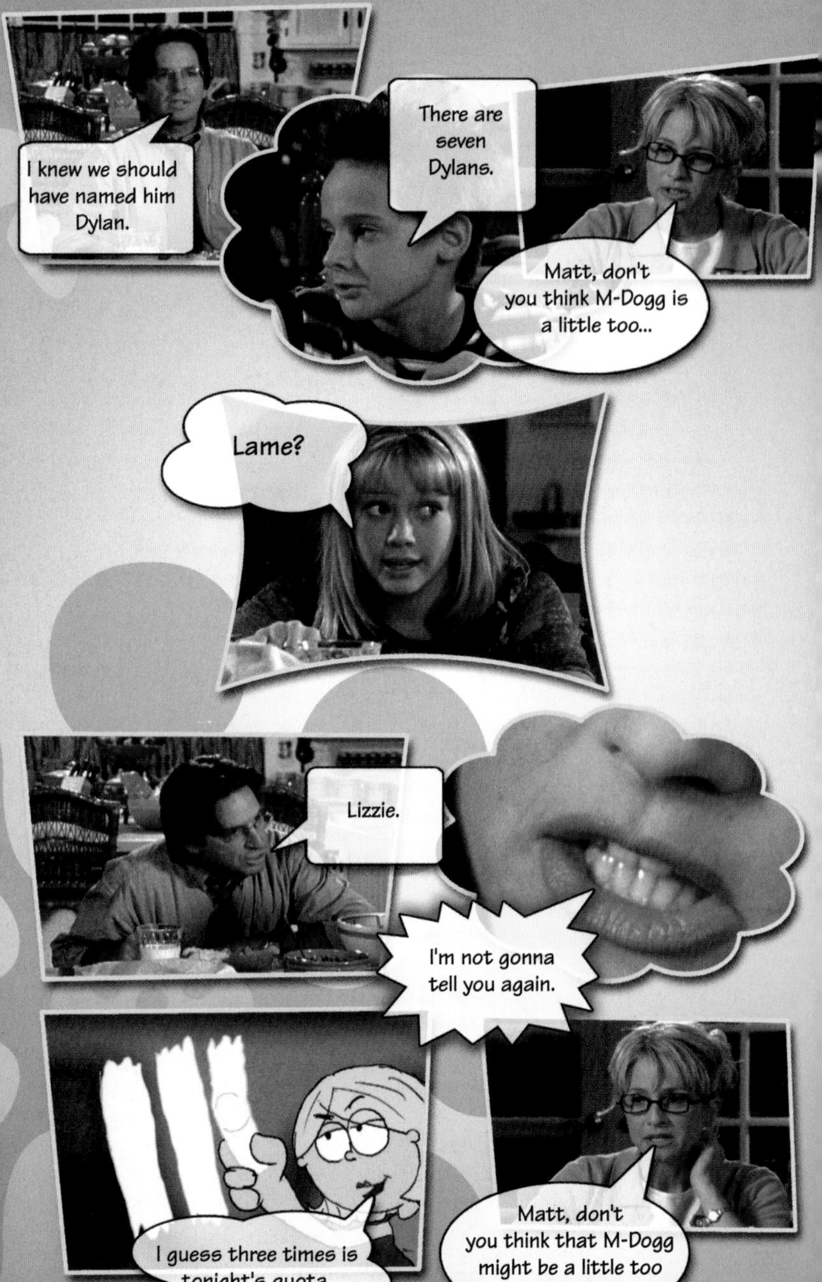
I knew we should have named him Dylan.
There are seven Dylans.
Matt, don't you think M-Dogg is a little too...
Lame?
Lizzie.
I'm not gonna tell you again.
I guess three times is tonight's quota.
Matt, don't you think that M-Dogg might be a little too different?

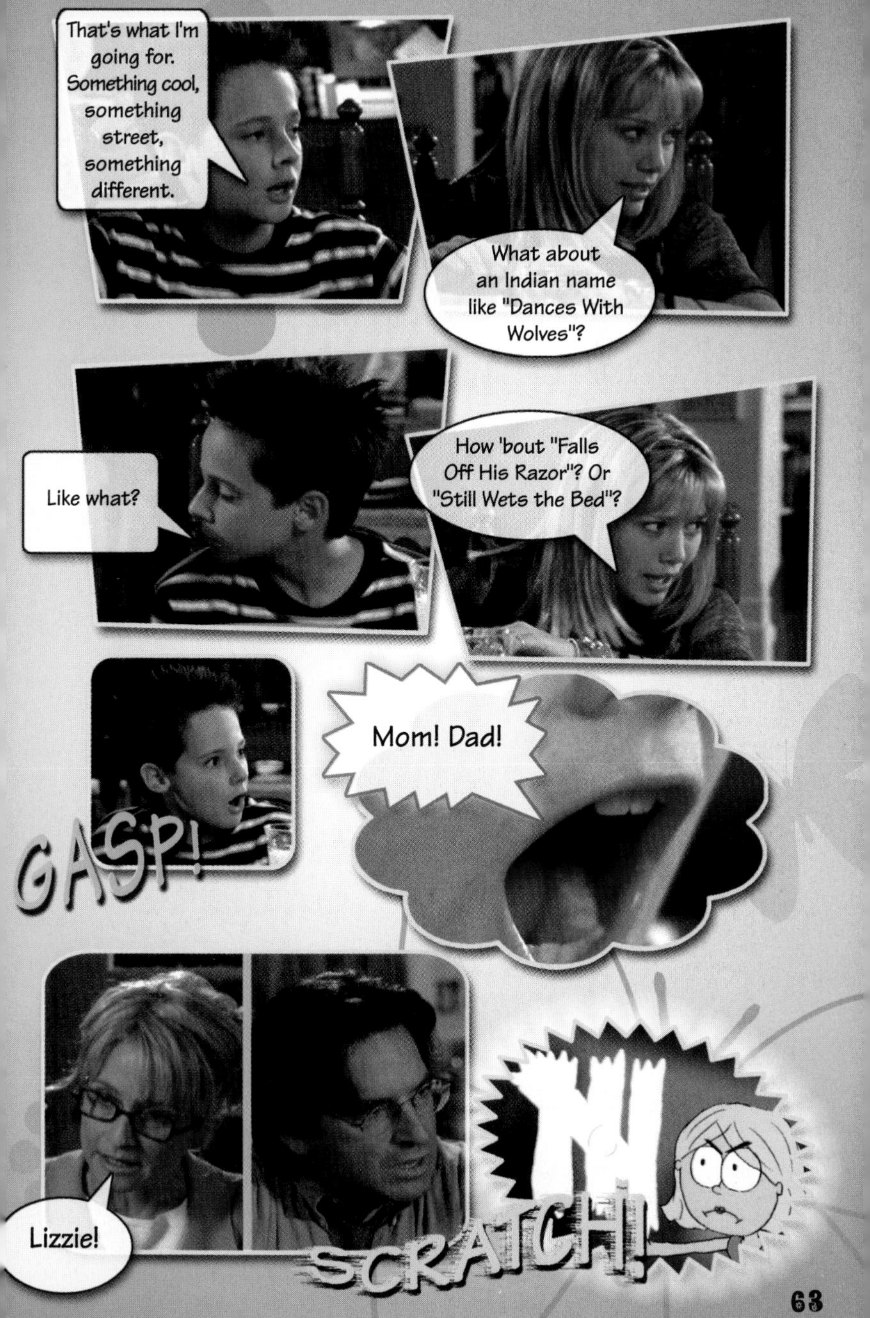

That's what I'm going for. Something cool, something street, something different.
What about an Indian name like "Dances With Wolves"?
Like what?
How 'bout "Falls Off His Razor"? Or "Still Wets the Bed"?
GASP!
Mom! Dad!
Lizzie!
SCRATCH!

THE NEXT DAY AT SCHOOL...

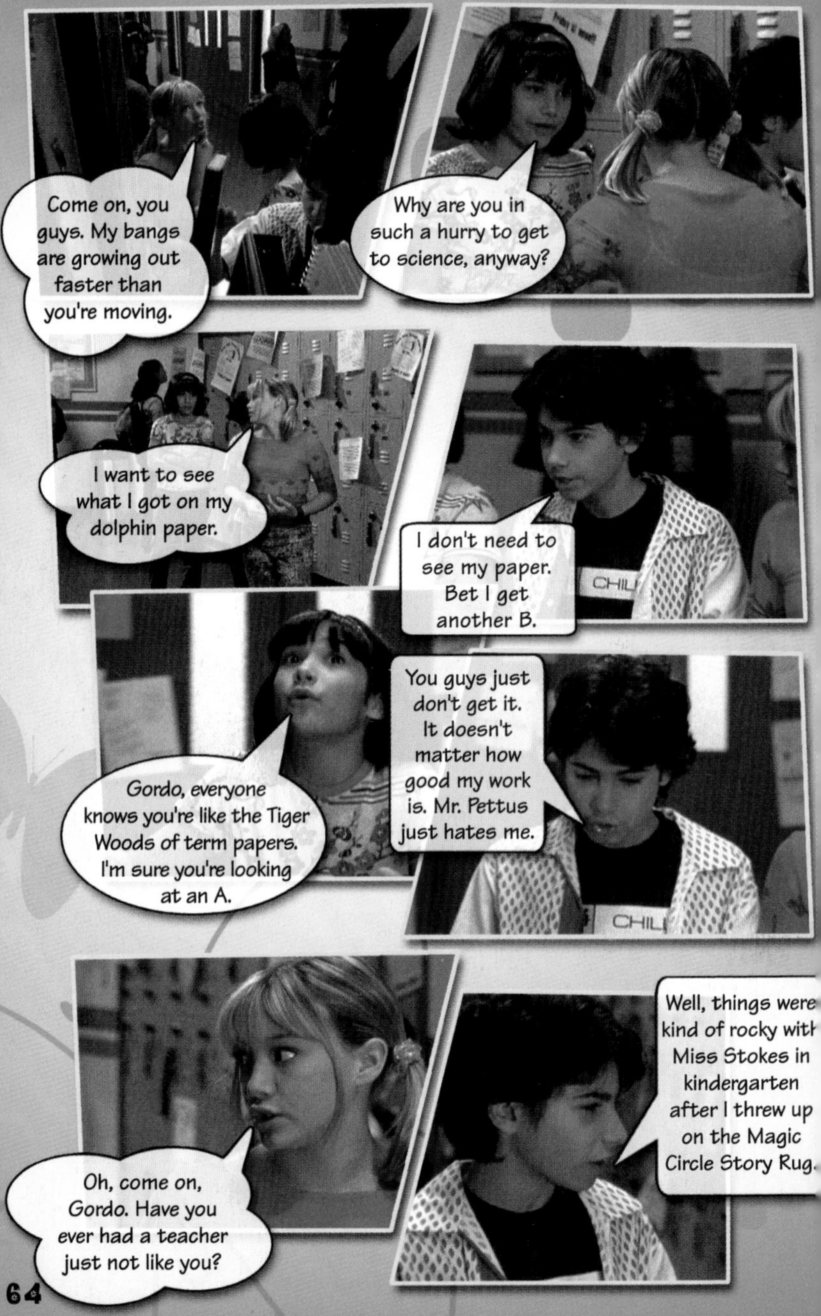

Come on, you guys. My bangs are growing out faster than you're moving.
Why are you in such a hurry to get to science, anyway?
I want to see what I got on my dolphin paper.
I don't need to see my paper. Bet I get another B.
Gordo, everyone knows you're like the Tiger Woods of term papers. I'm sure you're looking at an A.
You guys just don't get it. It doesn't matter how good my work is. Mr. Pettus just hates me.
Oh, come on, Gordo. Have you ever had a teacher just not like you?
Well, things were kind of rocky with Miss Stokes in kindergarten after I threw up on the Magic Circle Story Rug.

Oh, yeah! Yes! A B+! That's what I'm talkin' 'bout.

OUR FRIEND THE DOLPHIN

B+

By Lizzie Mc...

My dolphin paper! Okay, the margins were a little wide, but it had to be at least four pages. Go ahead, ask me what dolphins eat.

Okay, this is what I'm talking about.

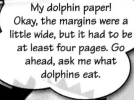

SEAWATER SALINITY AND DENSITY IN THE GULF STREAM

B

Gordo, this is amazing.

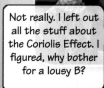

Not really. I left out all the stuff about the Coriolis Effect. I figured, why bother for a lousy B?

That grade has to be a mistake. This is an A+ paper.

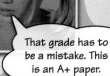

Maybe if it had your name on it.

If it had my name on it, it would be called "Our Friend the Ocean."

65

THE NEXT MORNING...

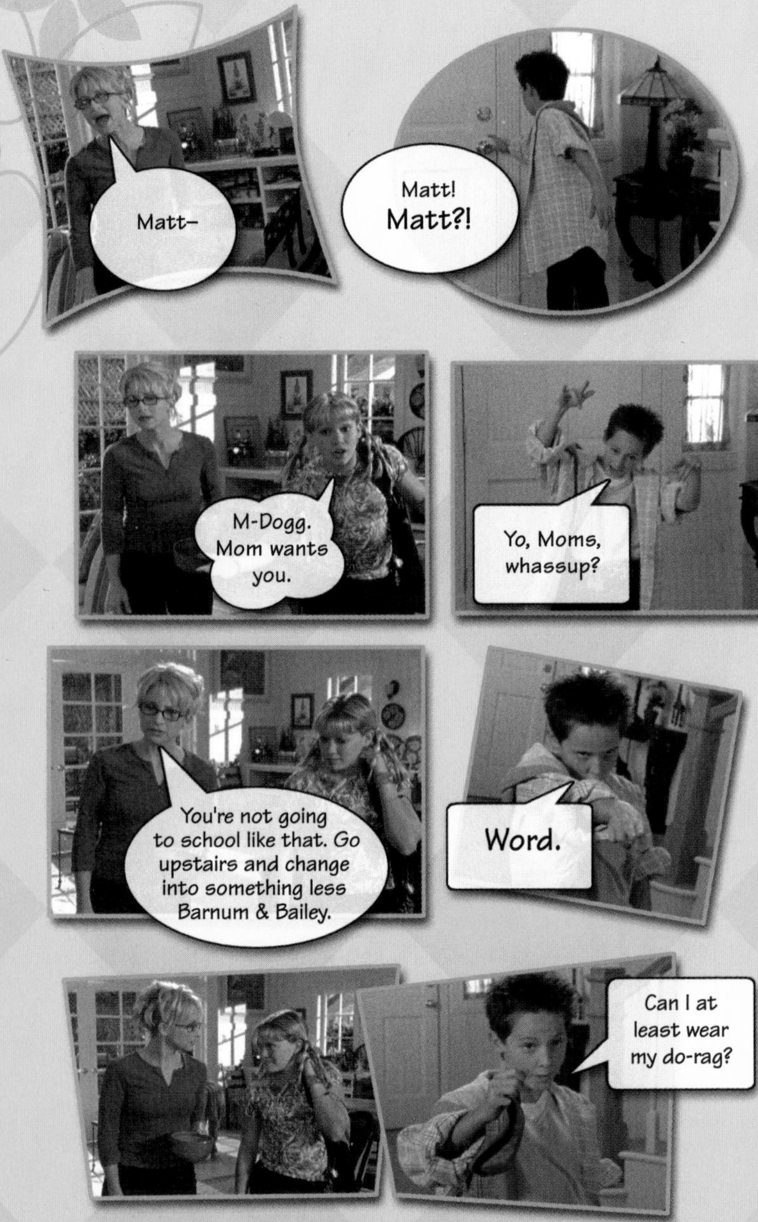
Matt–
Matt! Matt?!
M-Dogg. Mom wants you.
Yo, Moms, whassup?
You're not going to school like that. Go upstairs and change into something less Barnum & Bailey.
Word.
Can I at least wear my do-rag?

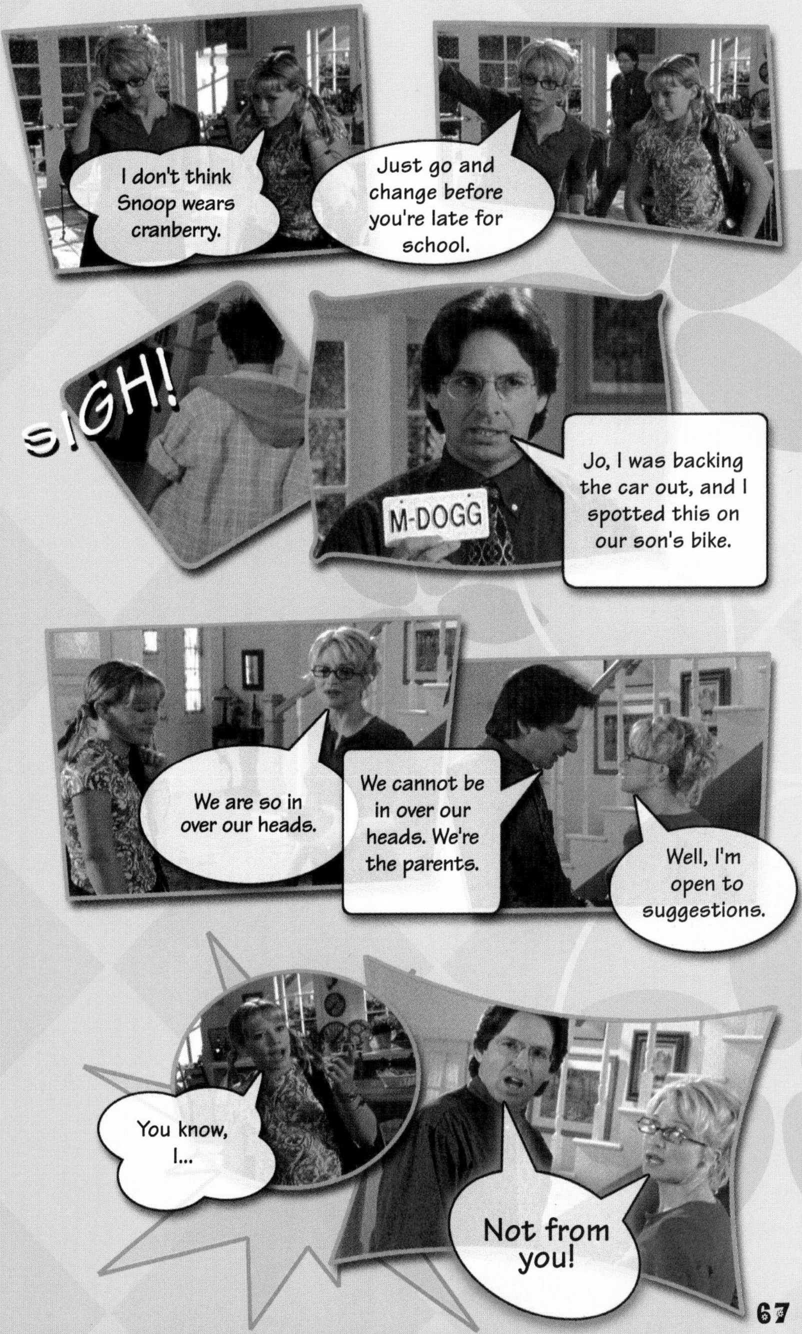
I don't think Snoop wears cranberry.
Just go and change before you're late for school.
SIGH!
M-DOGG
Jo, I was backing the car out, and I spotted this on our son's bike.
We are so in over our heads.
We cannot be in over our heads. We're the parents.
Well, I'm open to suggestions.
You know, I...
Not from you!

IN SCIENCE CLASS AGAIN...

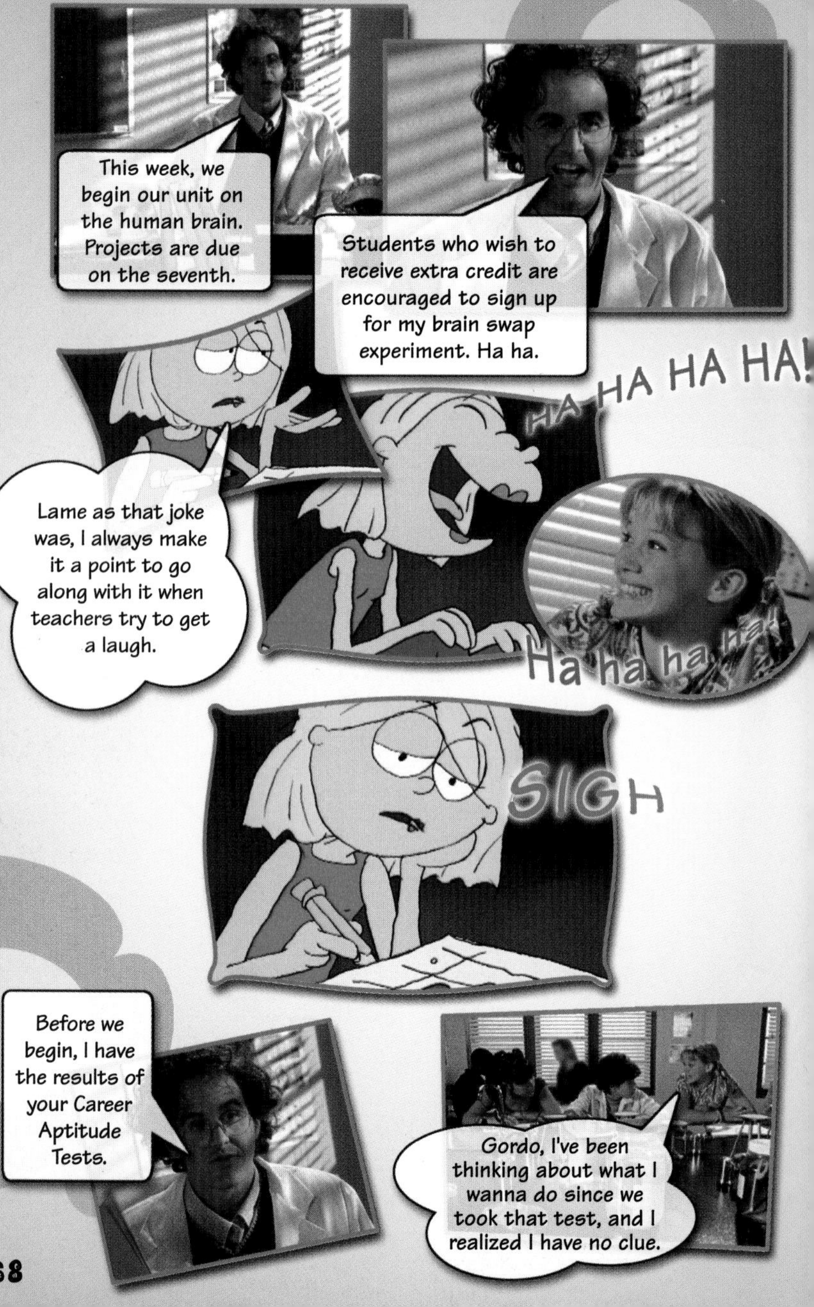
This week, we begin our unit on the human brain. Projects are due on the seventh.
Students who wish to receive extra credit are encouraged to sign up for my brain swap experiment. Ha ha.
Lame as that joke was, I always make it a point to go along with it when teachers try to get a laugh.
HA HA HA HA!
Ha ha ha ha!
SIGH
Before we begin, I have the results of your Career Aptitude Tests.
Gordo, I've been thinking about what I wanna do since we took that test, and I realized I have no clue.

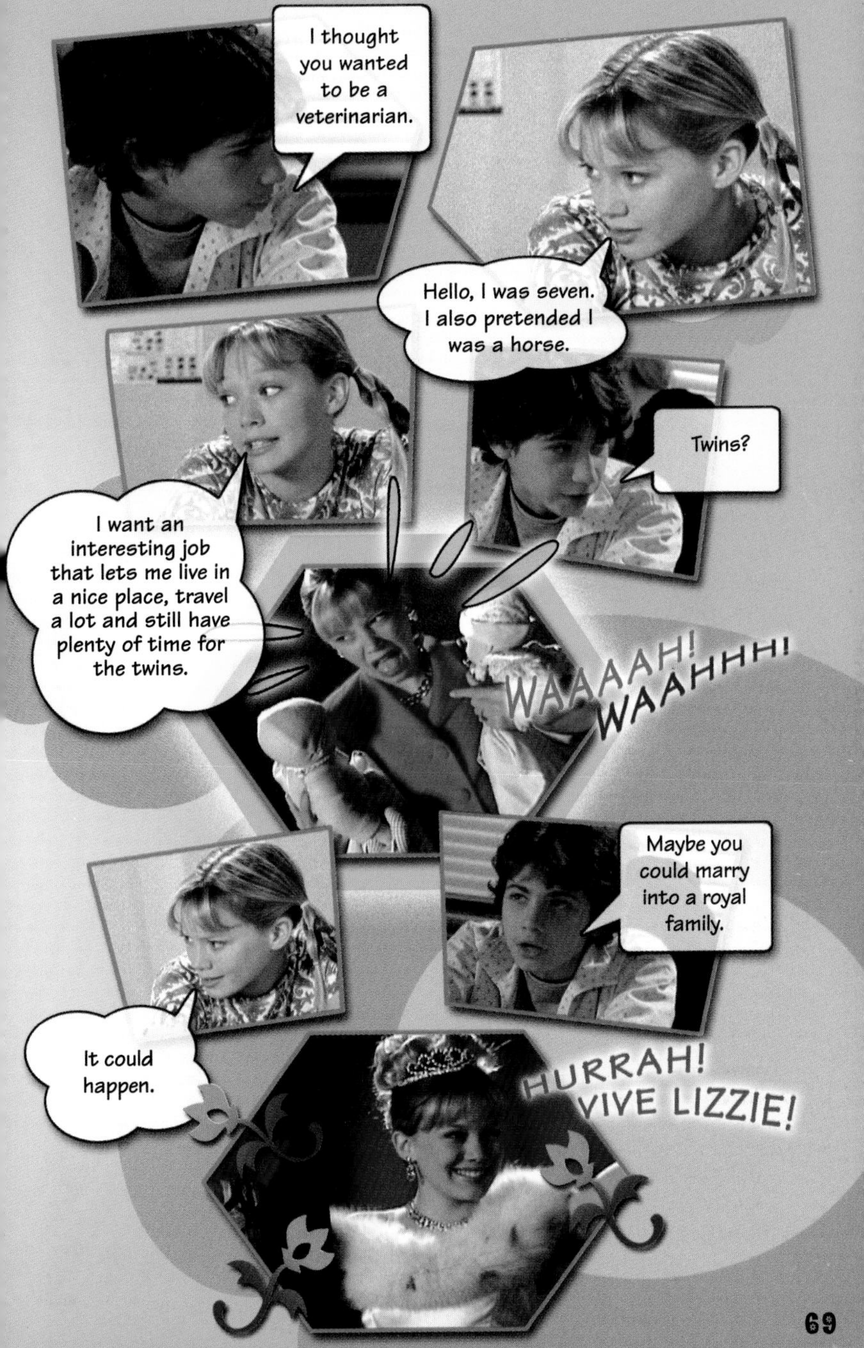
I thought you wanted to be a veterinarian.
Hello, I was seven. I also pretended I was a horse.
I want an interesting job that lets me live in a nice place, travel a lot and still have plenty of time for the twins.
Twins?
WAAAAH! WAAHHHH!
Maybe you could marry into a royal family.
It could happen.
HURRAH! VIVE LIZZIE!

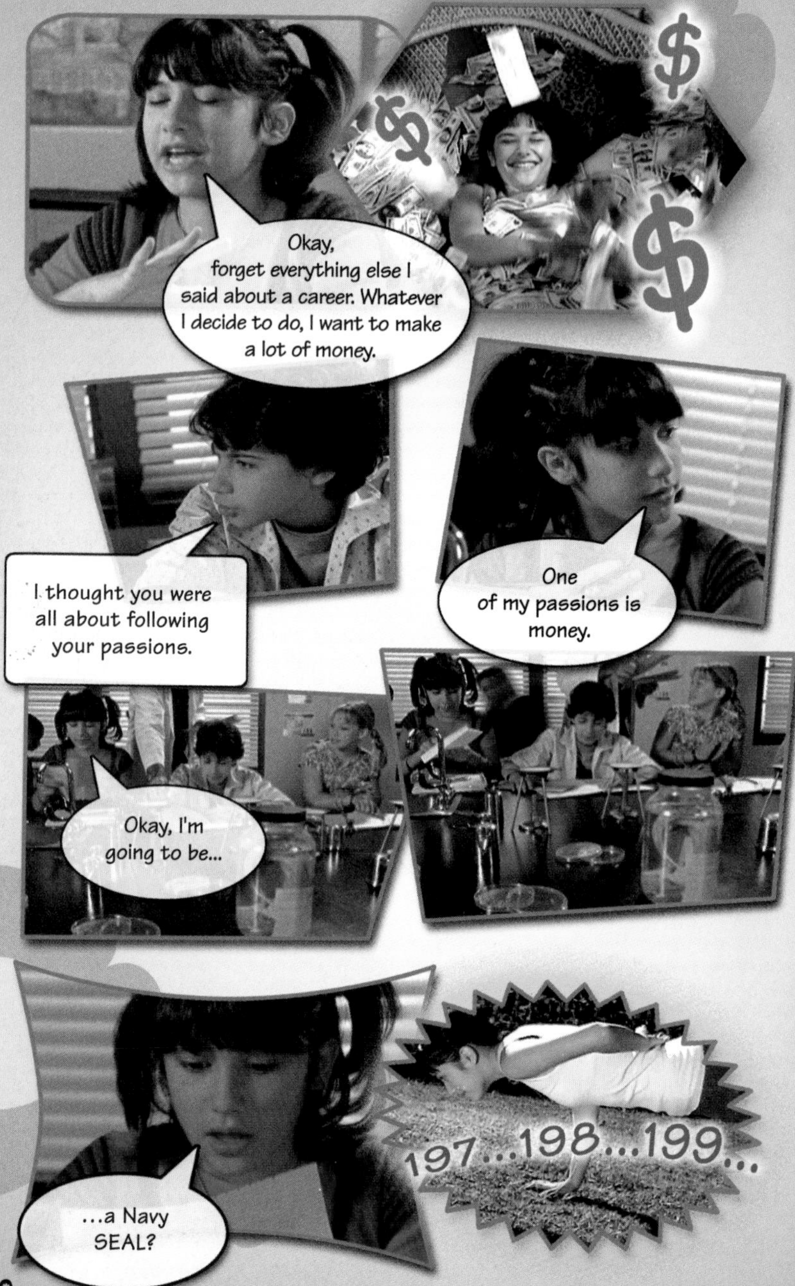
Okay, forget everything else I said about a career. Whatever I decide to do, I want to make a lot of money.
I thought you were all about following your passions.
One of my passions is money.
Okay, I'm going to be...
...a Navy SEAL?
197...198...199...

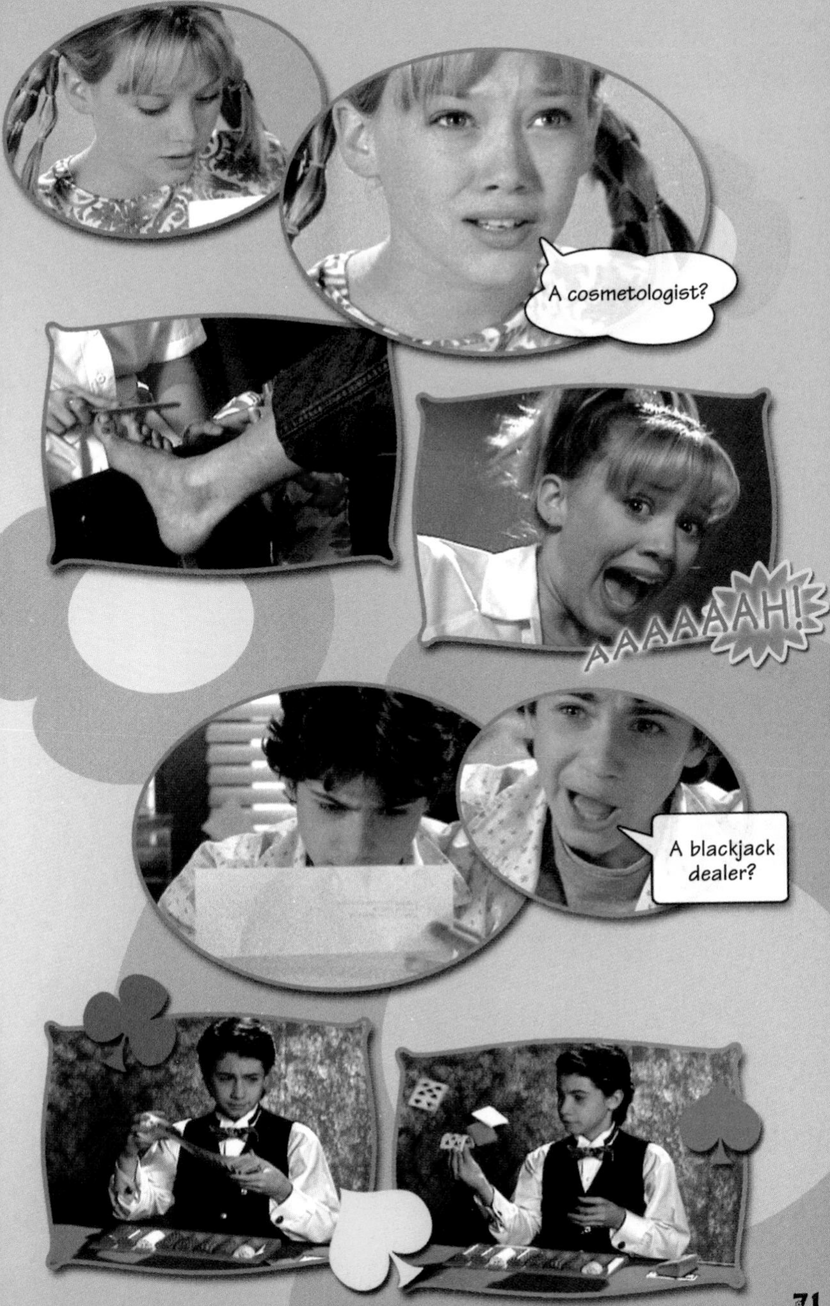
A cosmetologist?
AAAAAAH!
A blackjack dealer?

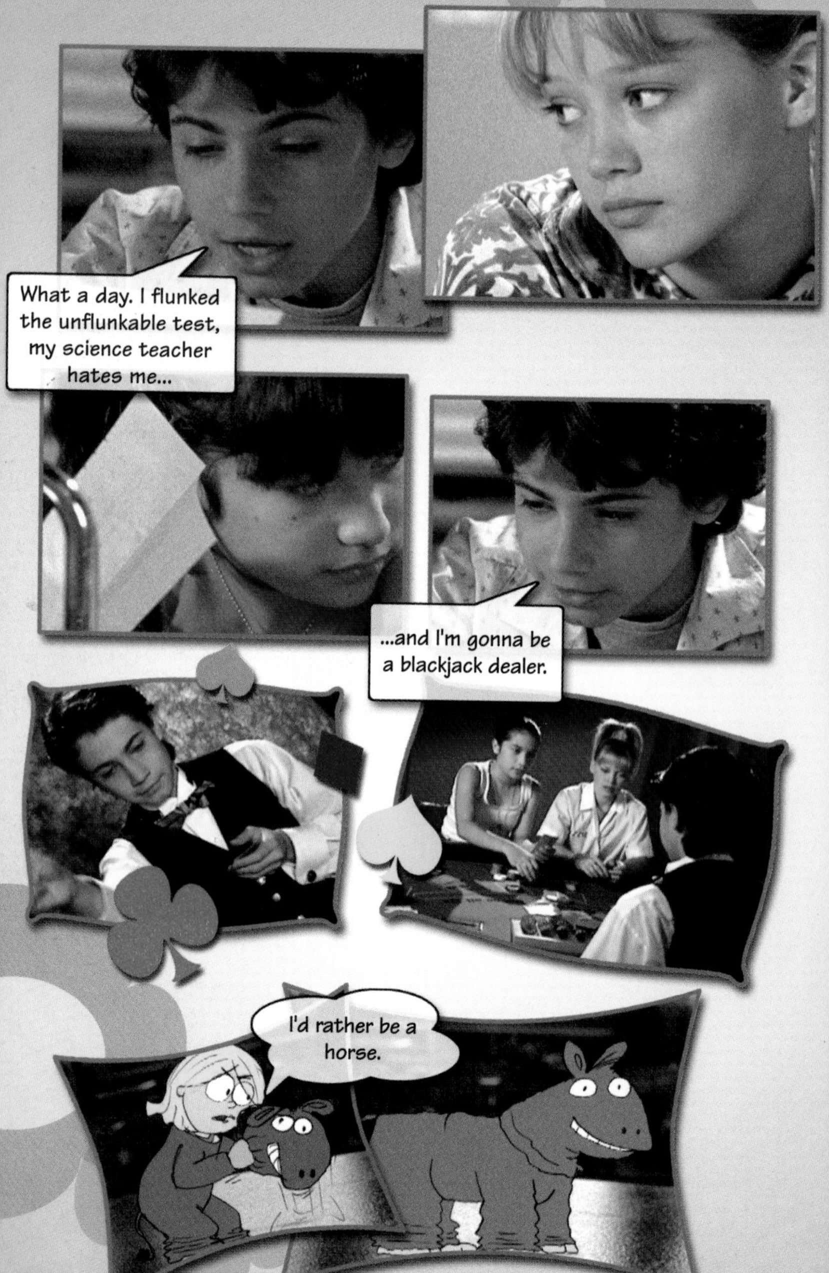
What a day. I flunked the unflunkable test, my science teacher hates me...
...and I'm gonna be a blackjack dealer.
I'd rather be a horse.

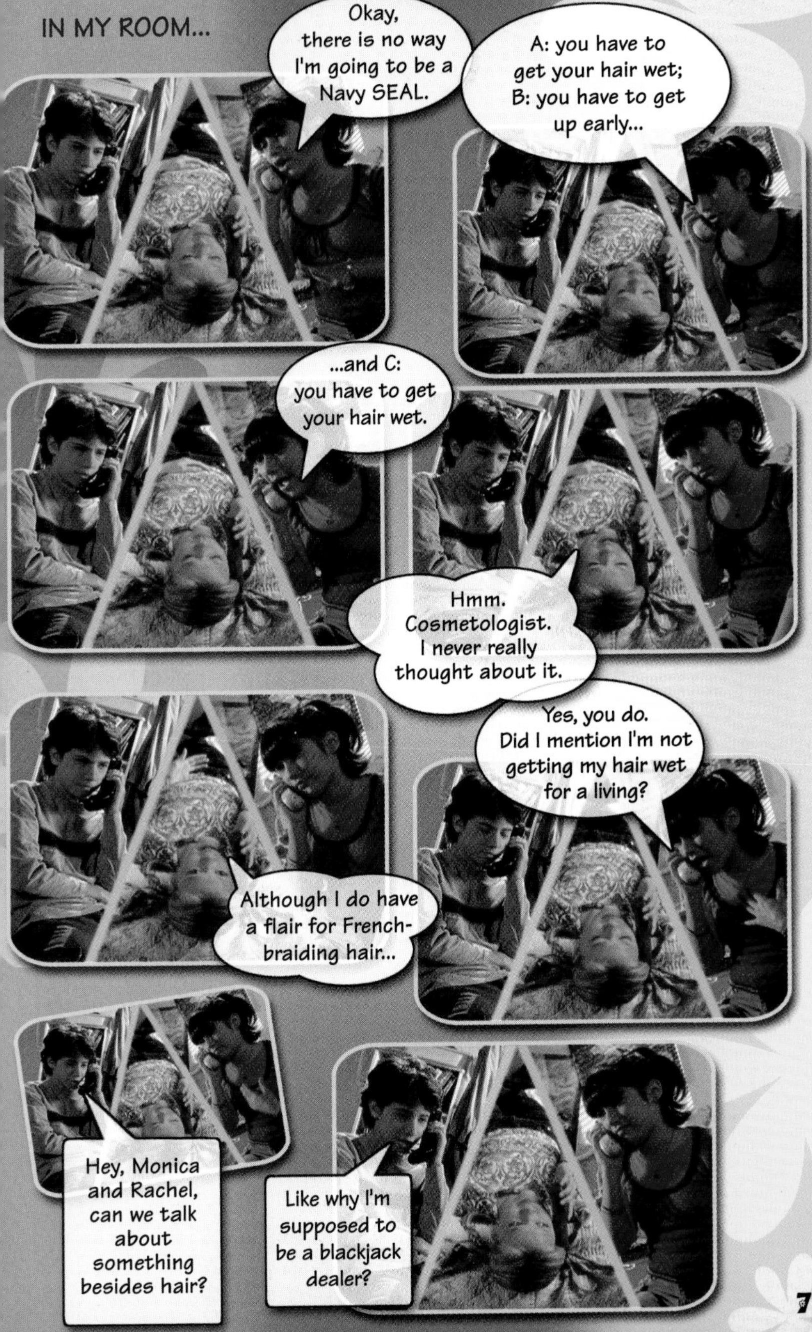
IN MY ROOM...
Okay, there is no way I'm going to be a Navy SEAL.
A: you have to get your hair wet; B: you have to get up early...
...and C: you have to get your hair wet.
Hmm. Cosmetologist. I never really thought about it.
Although I do have a flair for French-braiding hair...
Yes, you do. Did I mention I'm not getting my hair wet for a living?
Hey, Monica and Rachel, can we talk about something besides hair?
Like why I'm supposed to be a blackjack dealer?

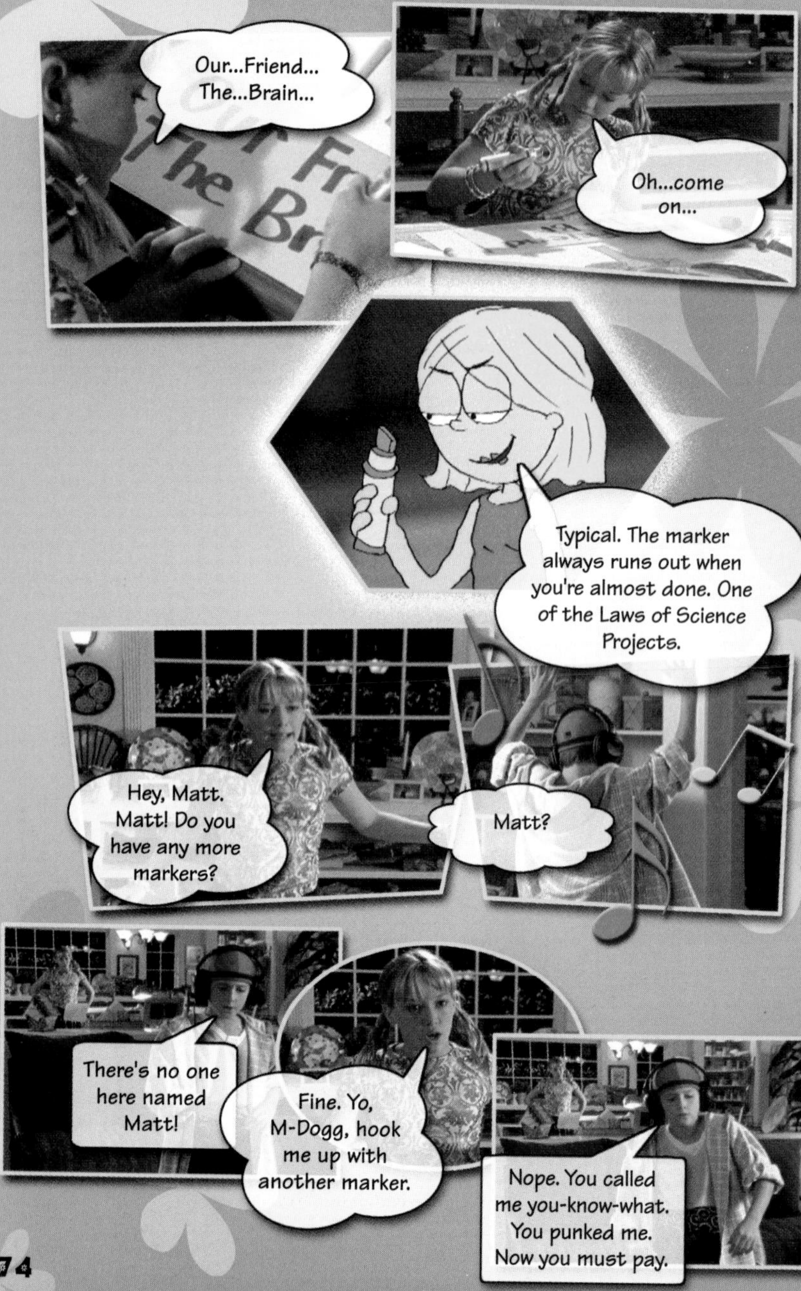
Our...Friend... The...Brain...
Oh...come on...
Typical. The marker always runs out when you're almost done. One of the Laws of Science Projects.
Hey, Matt. Matt! Do you have any more markers?
Matt?
There's no one here named Matt!
Fine. Yo, M-Dogg, hook me up with another marker.
Nope. You called me you-know-what. You punked me. Now you must pay.

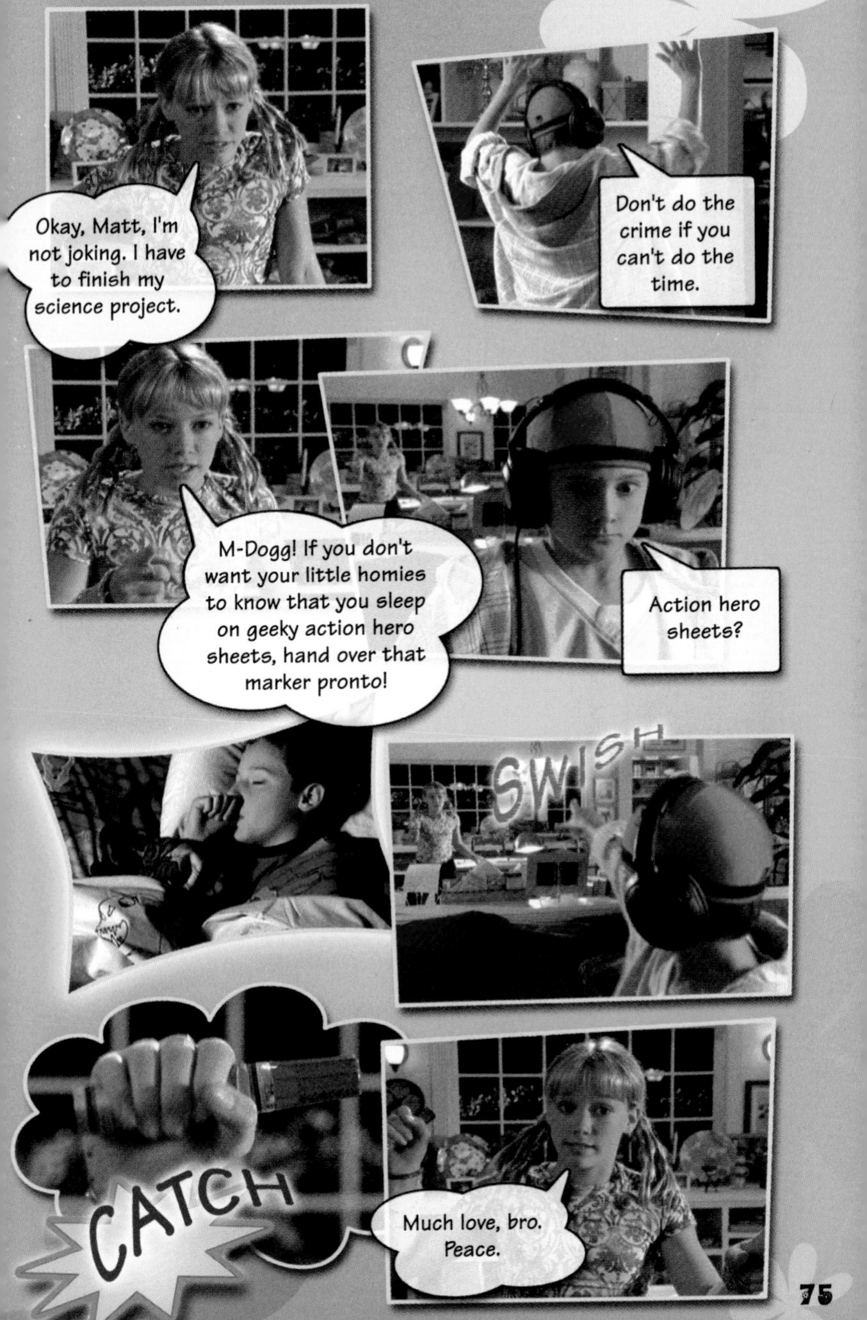
Okay, Matt, I'm not joking. I have to finish my science project.
Don't do the crime if you can't do the time.
M-Dogg! If you don't want your little homies to know that you sleep on geeky action hero sheets, hand over that marker pronto!
Action hero sheets?
SWISH
CATCH
Much love, bro. Peace.

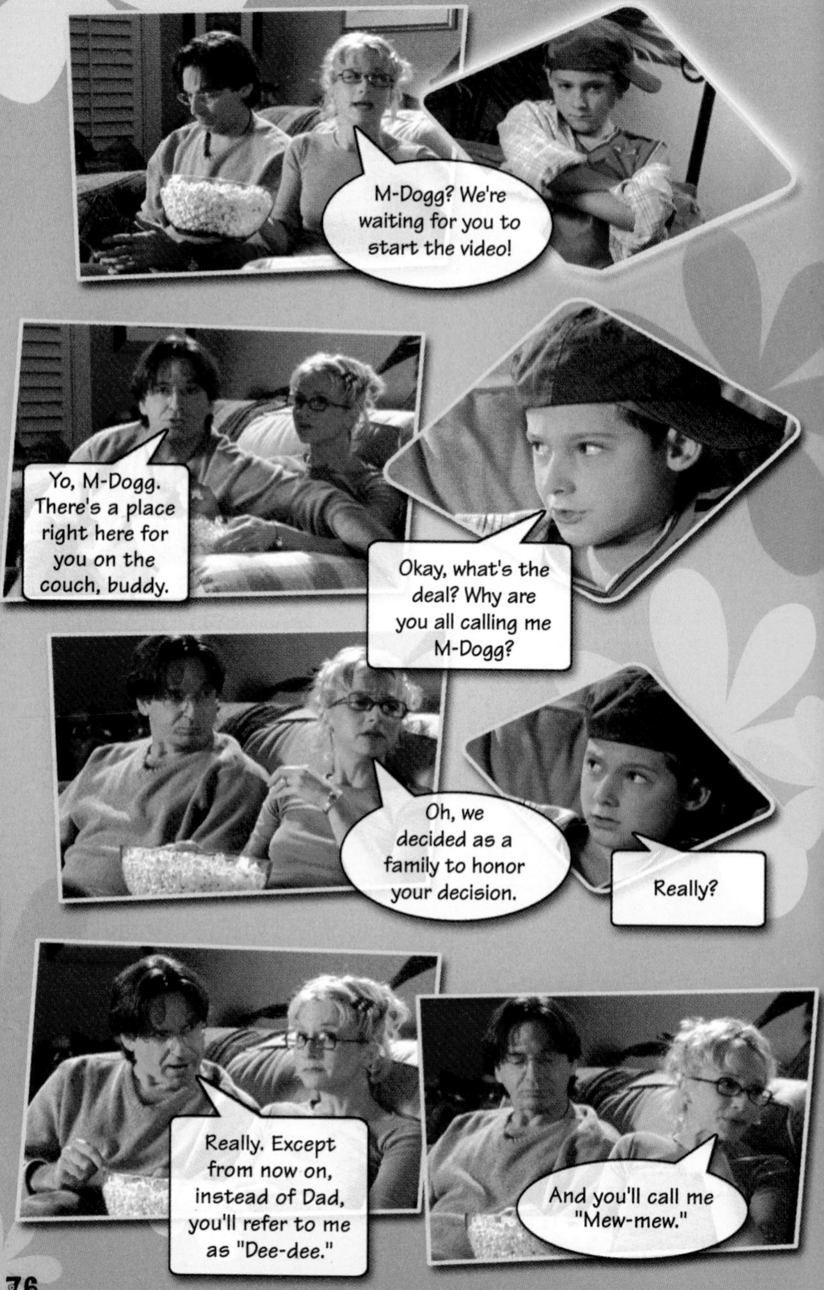
M-Dogg? We're waiting for you to start the video!
Yo, M-Dogg. There's a place right here for you on the couch, buddy.
Okay, what's the deal? Why are you all calling me M-Dogg?
Oh, we decided as a family to honor your decision.
Really?
Really. Except from now on, instead of Dad, you'll refer to me as "Dee-dee."
And you'll call me "Mew-mew."

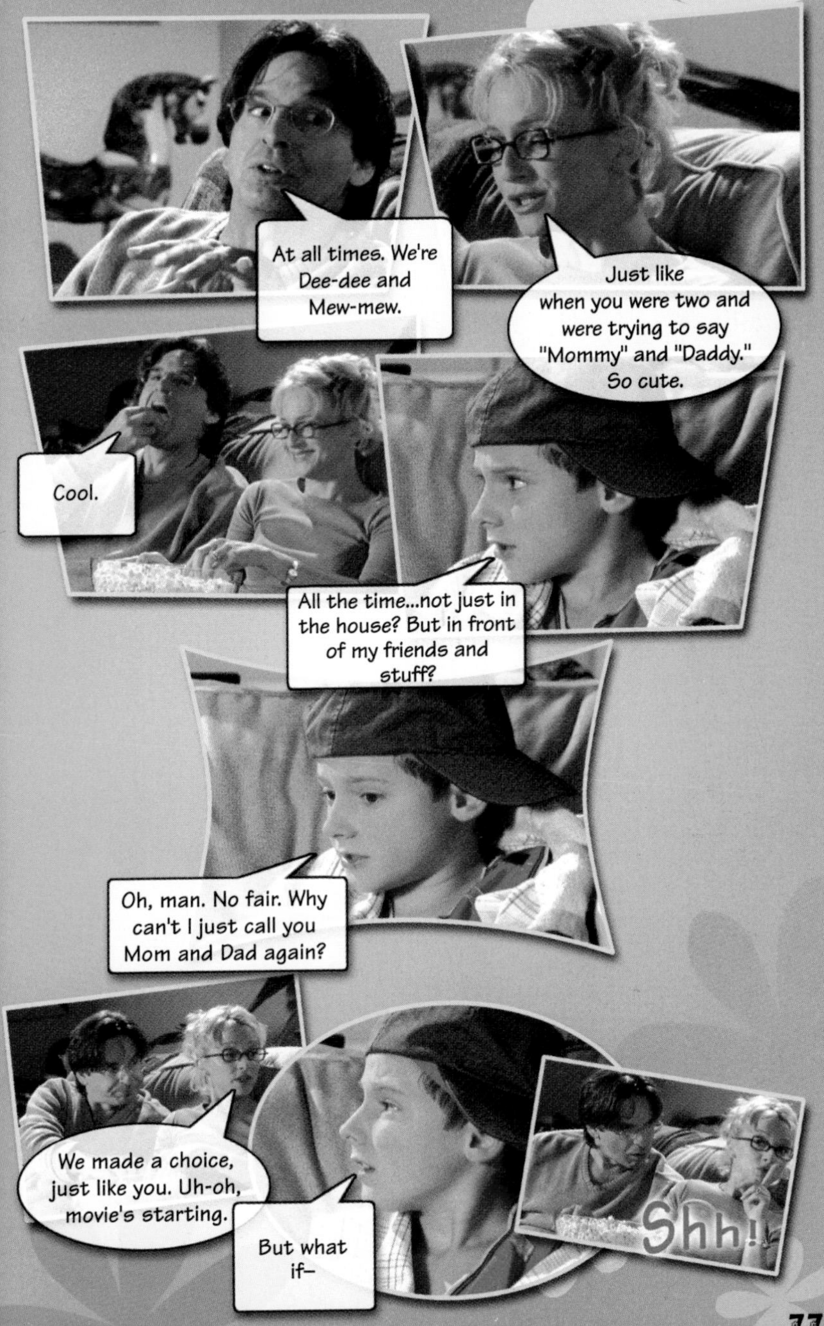
At all times. We're Dee-dee and Mew-mew.
Just like when you were two and were trying to say "Mommy" and "Daddy." So cute.
Cool.
All the time...not just in the house? But in front of my friends and stuff?
Oh, man. No fair. Why can't I just call you Mom and Dad again?
We made a choice, just like you. Uh-oh, movie's starting.
But what if–
Shh!

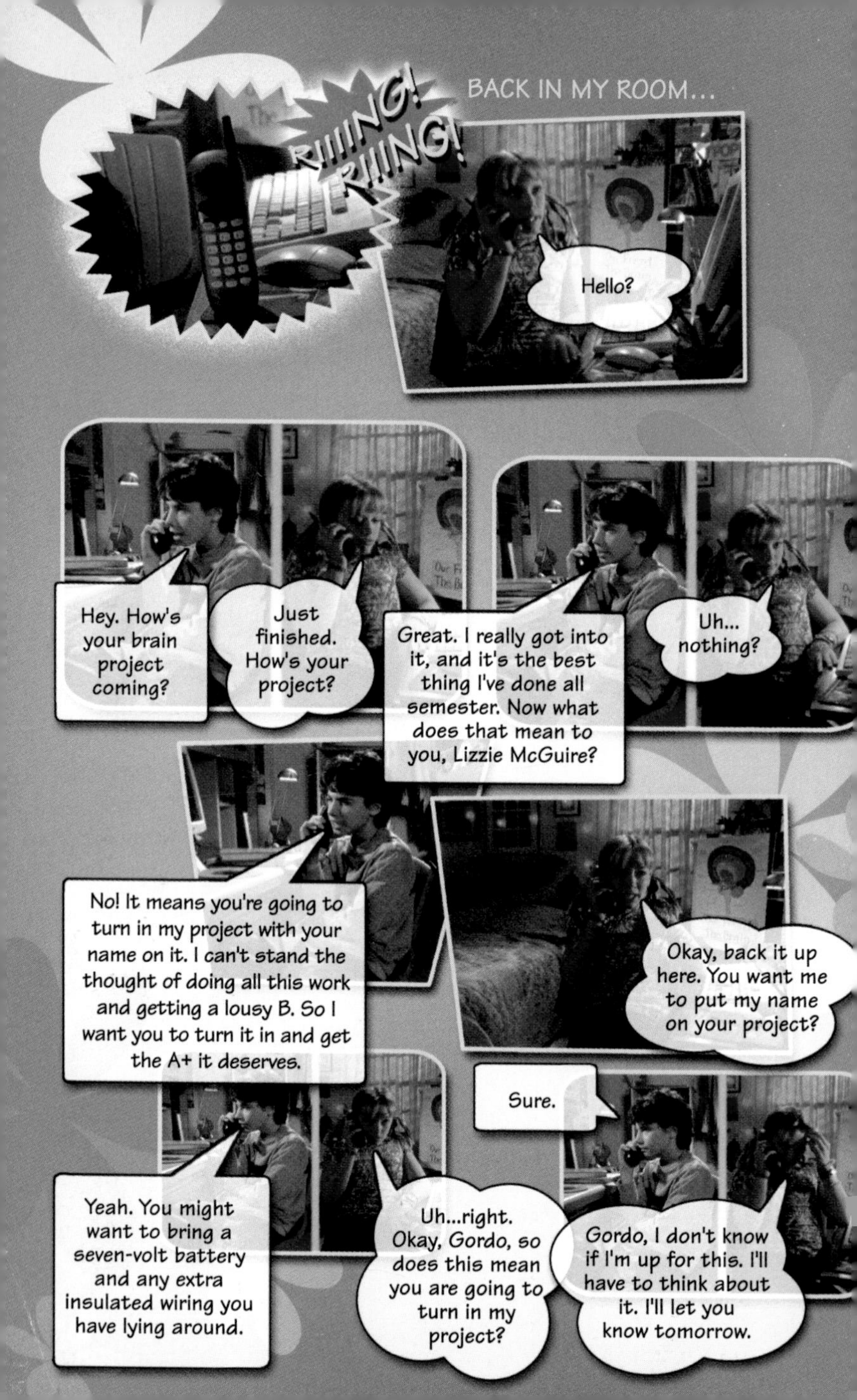
RIIIING! RIIIING!
BACK IN MY ROOM...
Hello?
Hey. How's your brain project coming?
Just finished. How's your project?
Great. I really got into it, and it's the best thing I've done all semester. Now what does that mean to you, Lizzie McGuire?
Uh... nothing?
No! It means you're going to turn in my project with your name on it. I can't stand the thought of doing all this work and getting a lousy B. So I want you to turn it in and get the A+ it deserves.
Okay, back it up here. You want me to put my name on your project?
Yeah. You might want to bring a seven-volt battery and any extra insulated wiring you have lying around.
Uh...right. Okay, Gordo, so does this mean you are going to turn in my project?
Sure.
Gordo, I don't know if I'm up for this. I'll have to think about it. I'll let you know tomorrow.

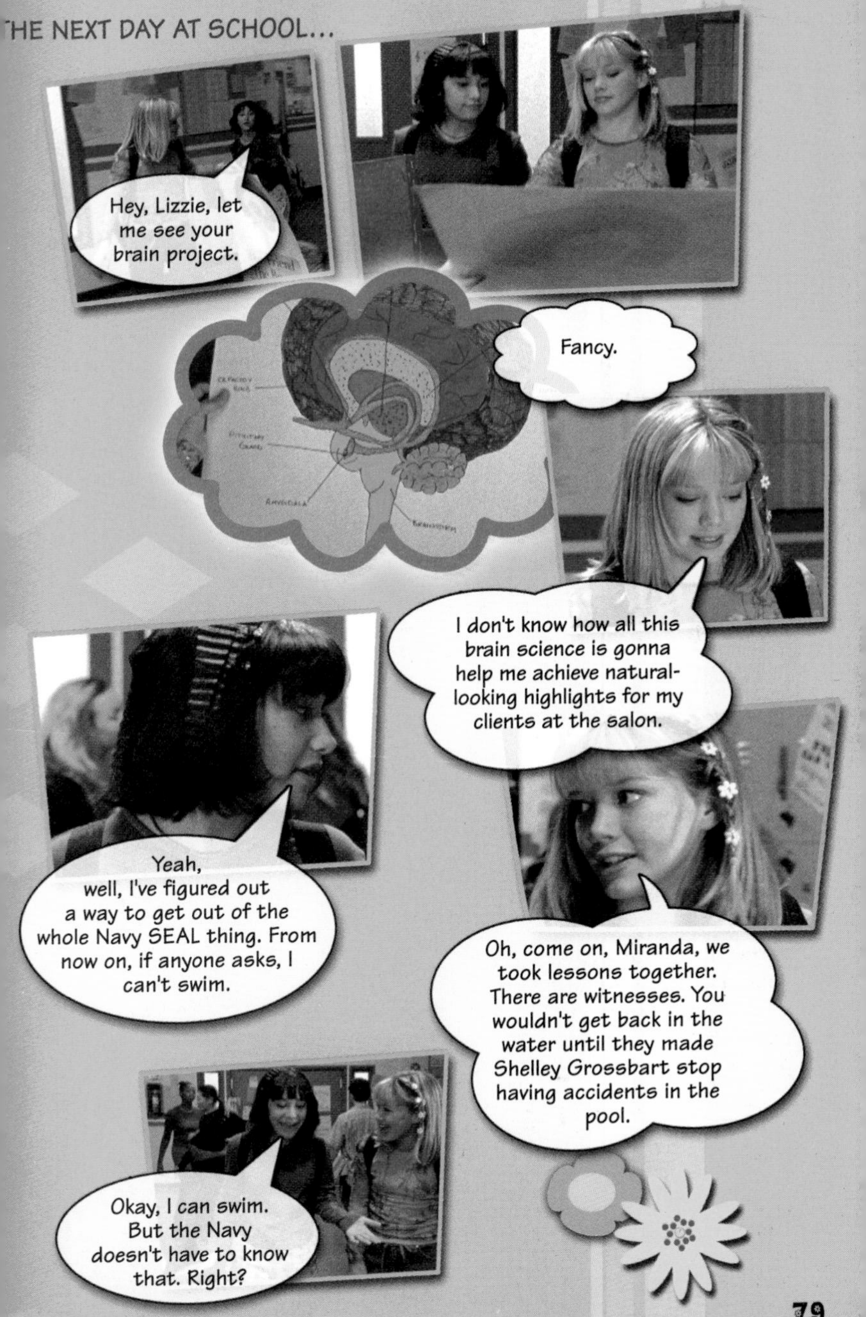
THE NEXT DAY AT SCHOOL...
Hey, Lizzie, let me see your brain project.
Fancy.
I don't know how all this brain science is gonna help me achieve natural-looking highlights for my clients at the salon.
Yeah, well, I've figured out a way to get out of the whole Navy SEAL thing. From now on, if anyone asks, I can't swim.
Oh, come on, Miranda, we took lessons together. There are witnesses. You wouldn't get back in the water until they made Shelley Grossbart stop having accidents in the pool.
Okay, I can swim. But the Navy doesn't have to know that. Right?

Hey, guys.

Where's your project?

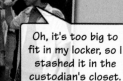

Oh, it's too big to fit in my locker, so I stashed it in the custodian's closet.

This must be some project.

Well, some people might think so. Others may only give it a B. But what difference does it make? I don't need straight A's. I'm just gonna be a blackjack dealer. You only have to count to 21.

Fine, you win. I'll switch projects with you.

You will?! Excellent! Come on, follow me.

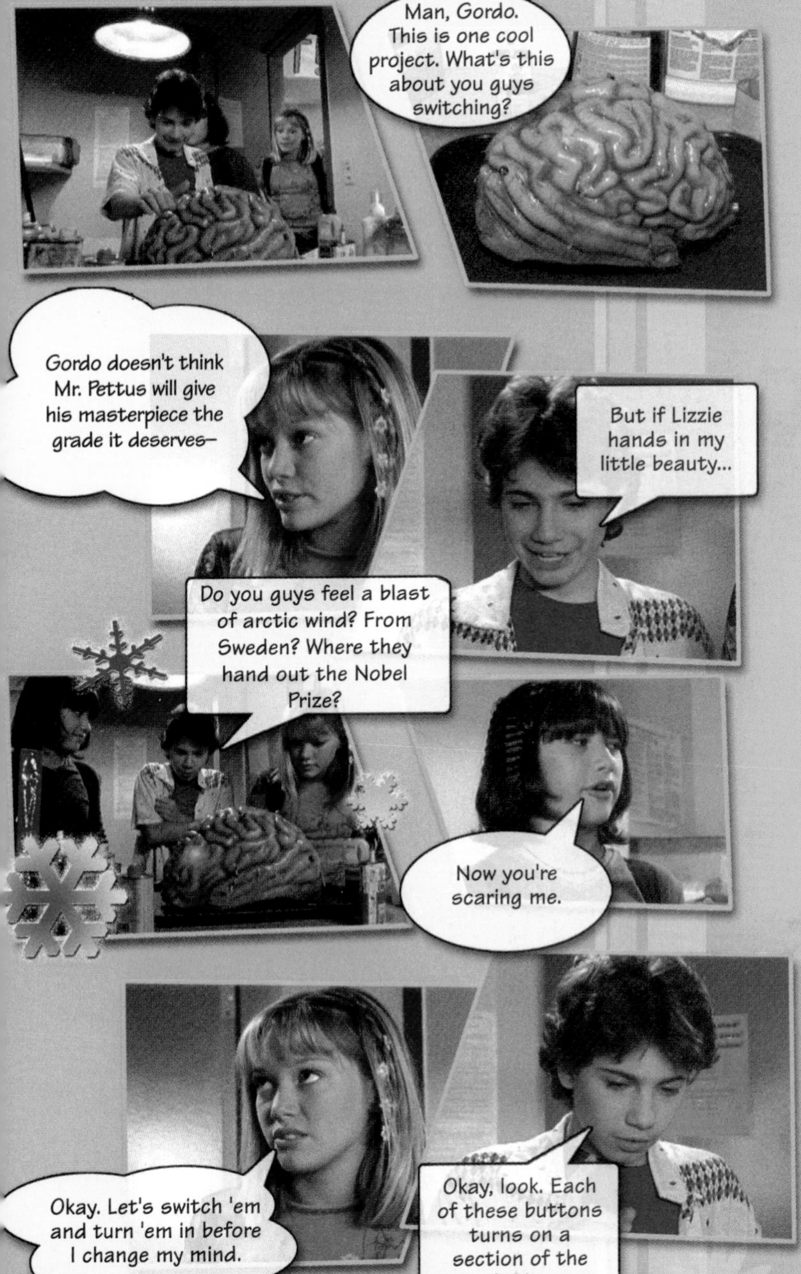
Man, Gordo. This is one cool project. What's this about you guys switching?
Gordo doesn't think Mr. Pettus will give his masterpiece the grade it deserves–
But if Lizzie hands in my little beauty...
Do you guys feel a blast of arctic wind? From Sweden? Where they hand out the Nobel Prize?
Now you're scaring me.
Okay. Let's switch 'em and turn 'em in before I change my mind.
Okay, look. Each of these buttons turns on a section of the brain.

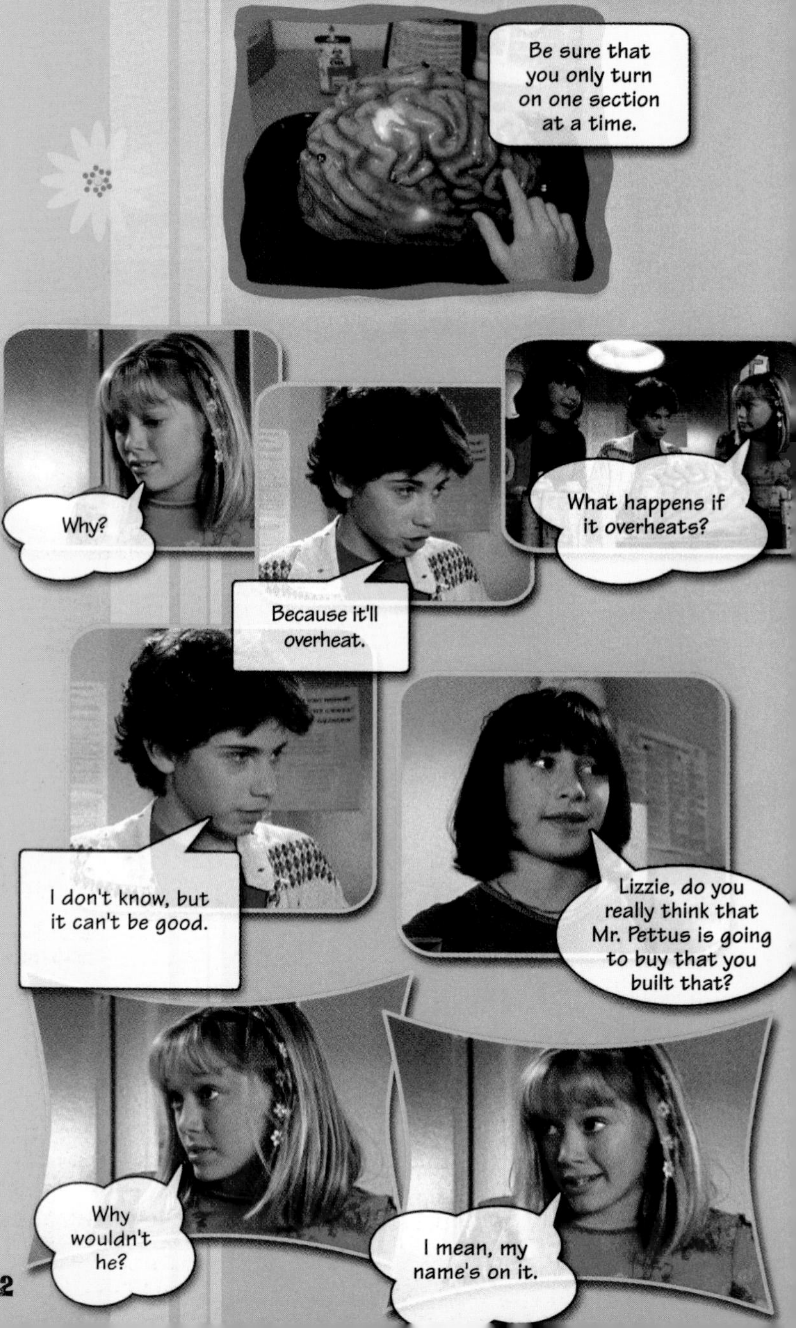

Be sure that you only turn on one section at a time.
Why?
Because it'll overheat.
What happens if it overheats?
I don't know, but it can't be good.
Lizzie, do you really think that Mr. Pettus is going to buy that you built that?
Why wouldn't he?
I mean, my name's on it.

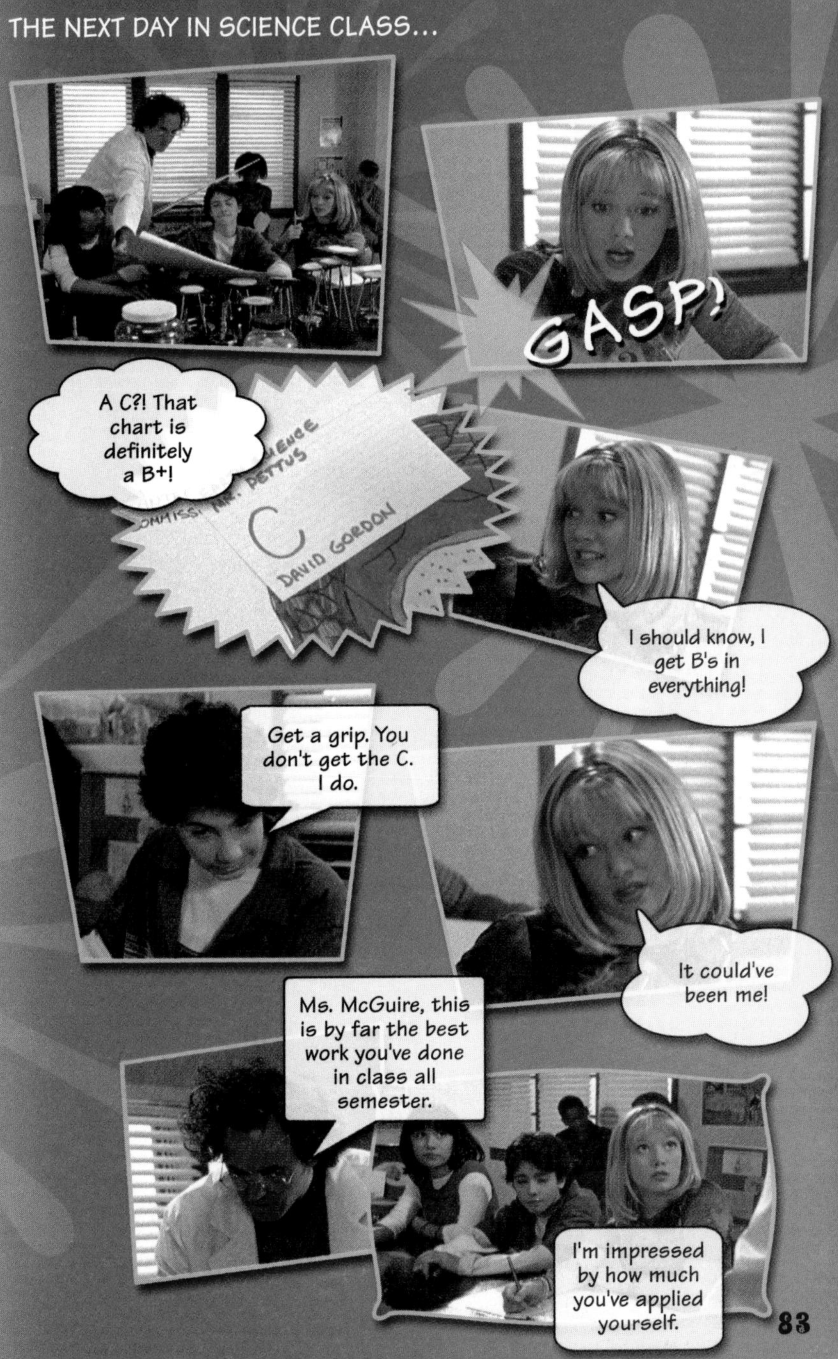
THE NEXT DAY IN SCIENCE CLASS...
GASP!
A C?! That chart is definitely a B+!
MR. PETTUS
C
DAVID GORDON
I should know, I get B's in everything!
Get a grip. You don't get the C. I do.
It could've been me!
Ms. McGuire, this is by far the best work you've done in class all semester.
I'm impressed by how much you've applied yourself.

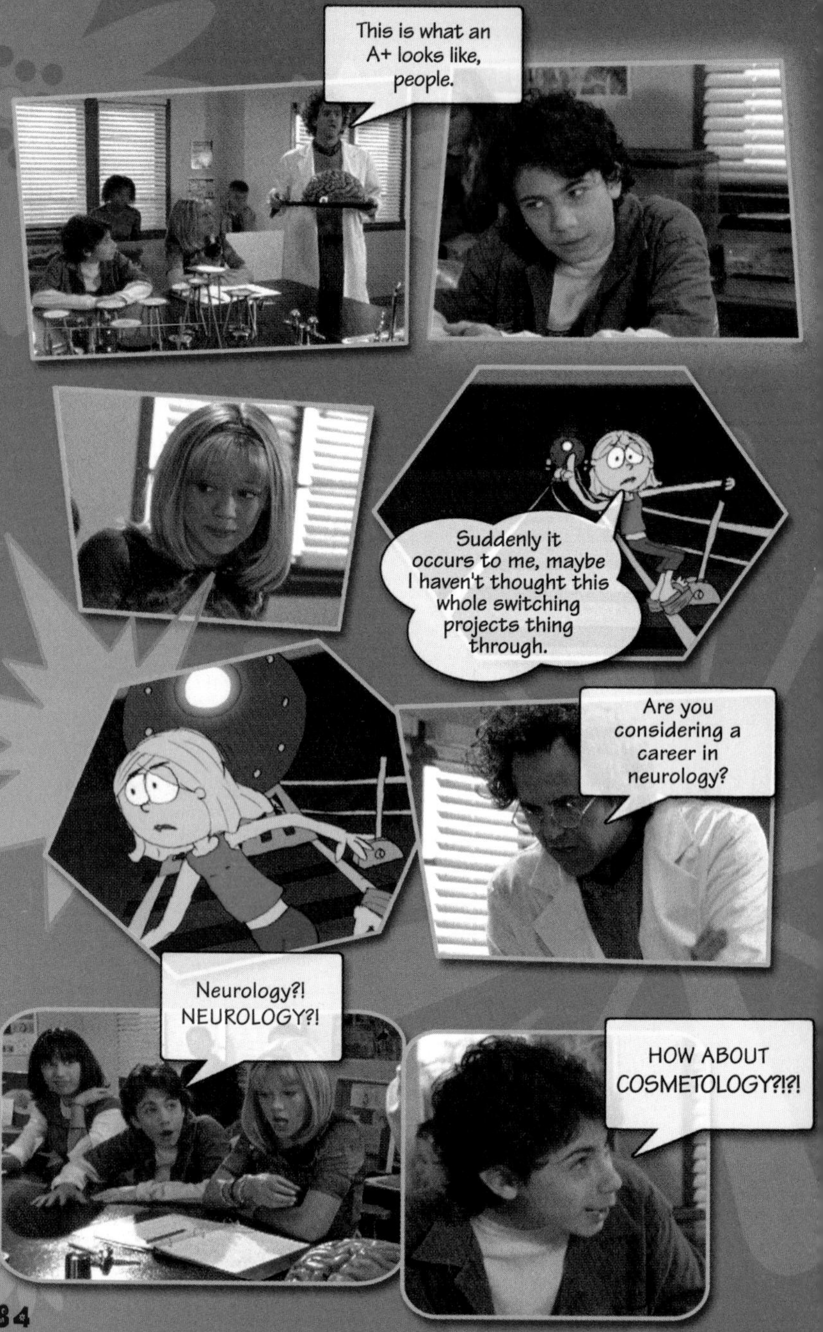

This is what an A+ looks like, people.
Suddenly it occurs to me, maybe I haven't thought this whole switching projects thing through.
Are you considering a career in neurology?
Neurology?! NEUROLOGY?!
HOW ABOUT COSMETOLOGY?!?!

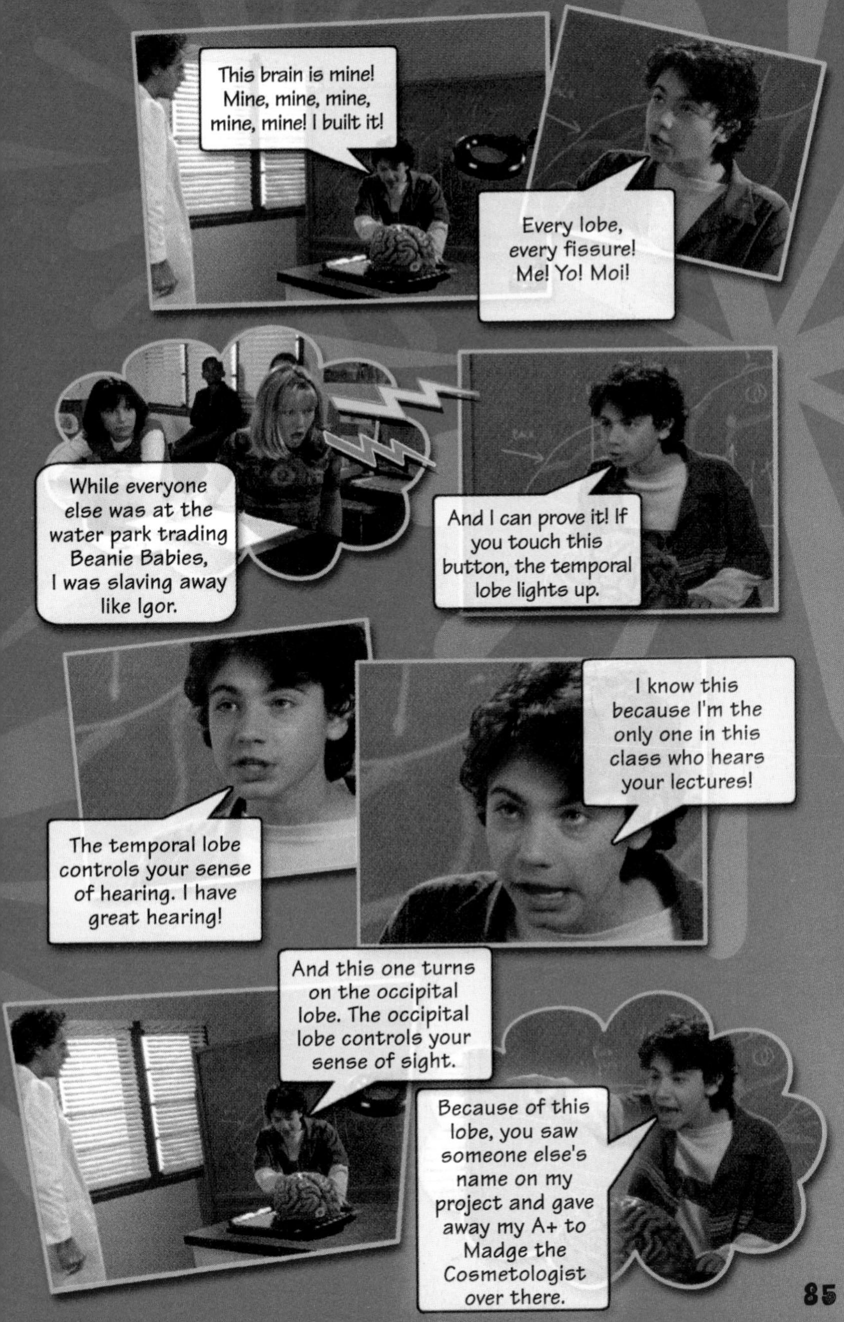
This brain is mine! Mine, mine, mine, mine, mine! I built it!
Every lobe, every fissure! Me! Yo! Moi!
While everyone else was at the water park trading Beanie Babies, I was slaving away like Igor.
And I can prove it! If you touch this button, the temporal lobe lights up.
The temporal lobe controls your sense of hearing. I have great hearing!
I know this because I'm the only one in this class who hears your lectures!
And this one turns on the occipital lobe. The occipital lobe controls your sense of sight.
Because of this lobe, you saw someone else's name on my project and gave away my A+ to Madge the Cosmetologist over there.

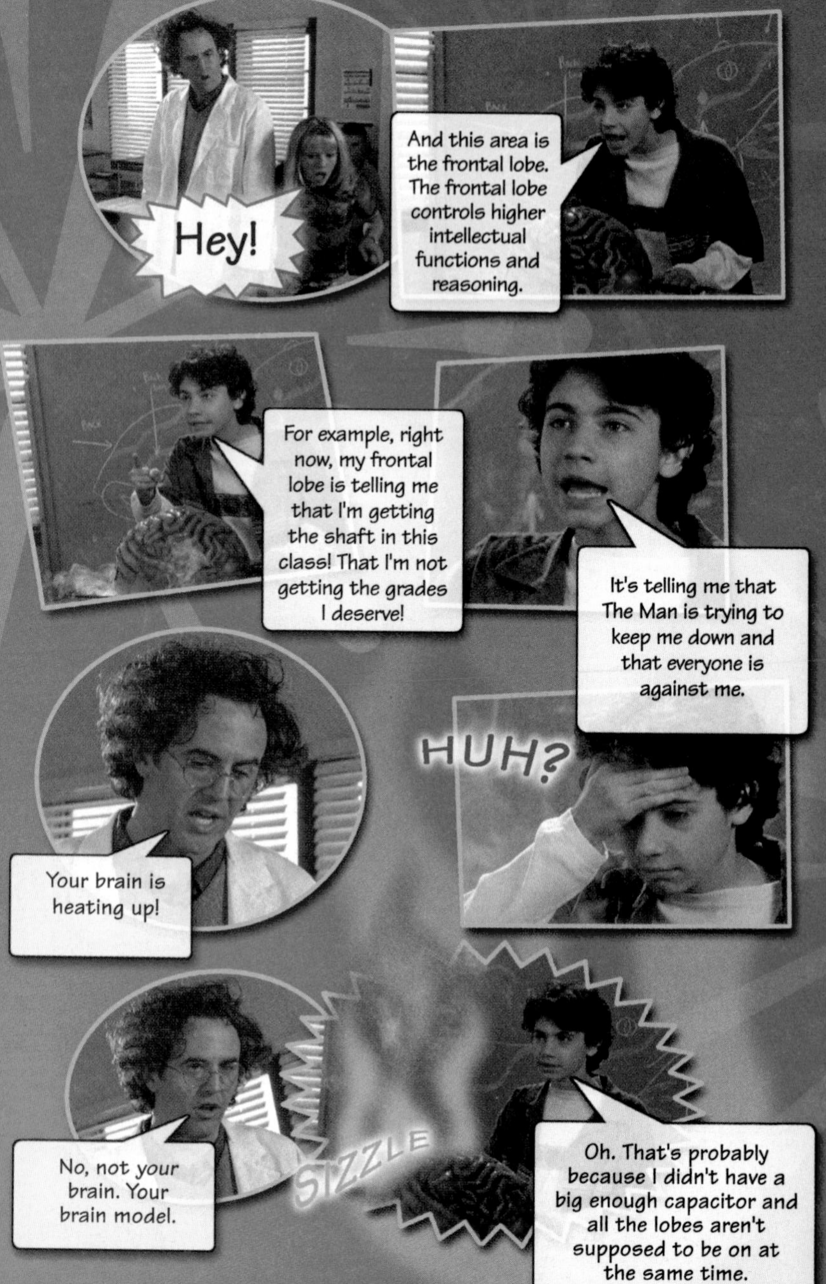
Hey!
And this area is the frontal lobe. The frontal lobe controls higher intellectual functions and reasoning.
For example, right now, my frontal lobe is telling me that I'm getting the shaft in this class! That I'm not getting the grades I deserve!
It's telling me that The Man is trying to keep me down and that everyone is against me.
Your brain is heating up!
HUH?
No, not your brain. Your brain model.
SIZZLE
Oh. That's probably because I didn't have a big enough capacitor and all the lobes aren't supposed to be on at the same time.

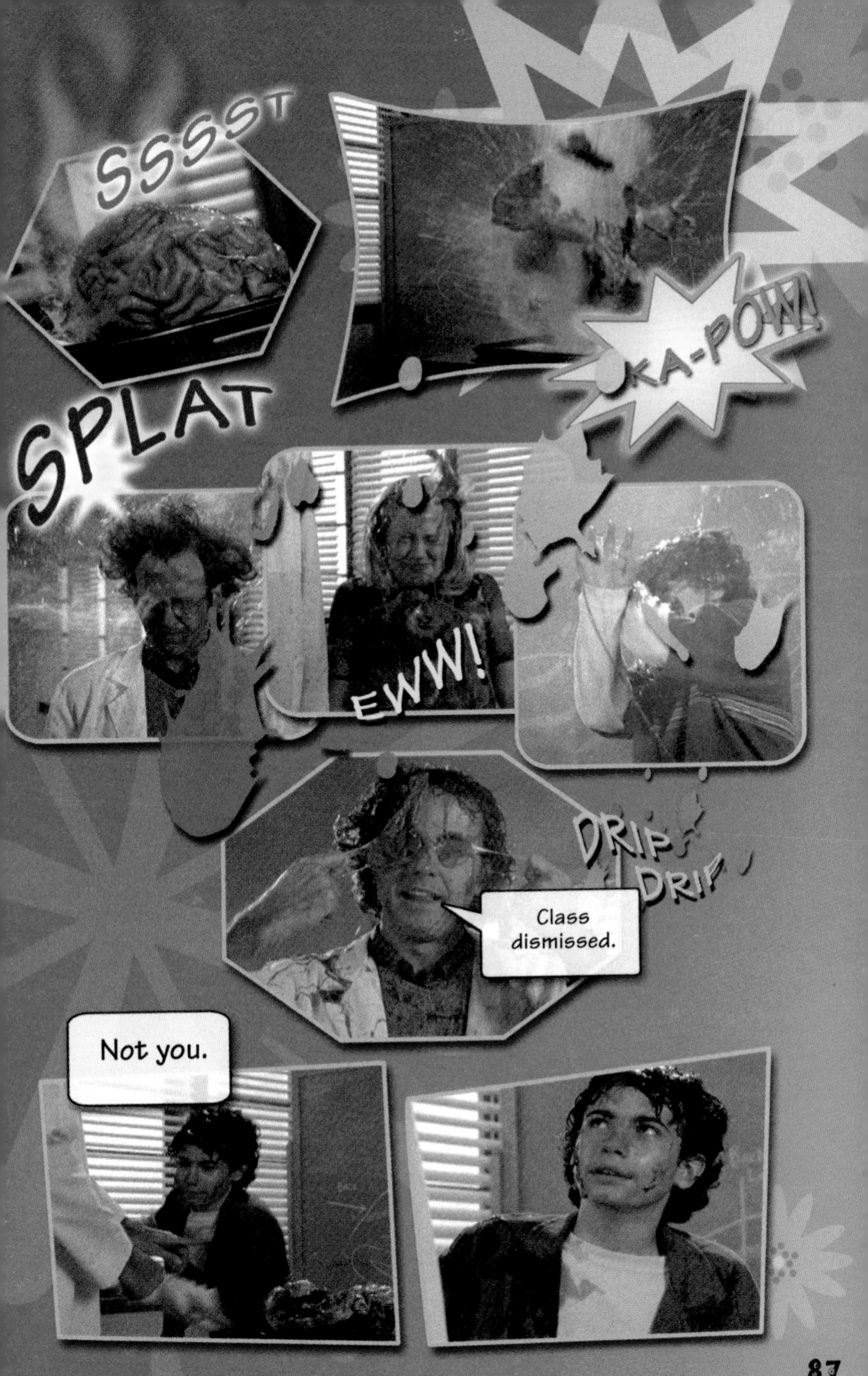
SSSST
KA-POW!
SPLAT
EWW!
DRIP
DRIP
Class dismissed.
Not you.

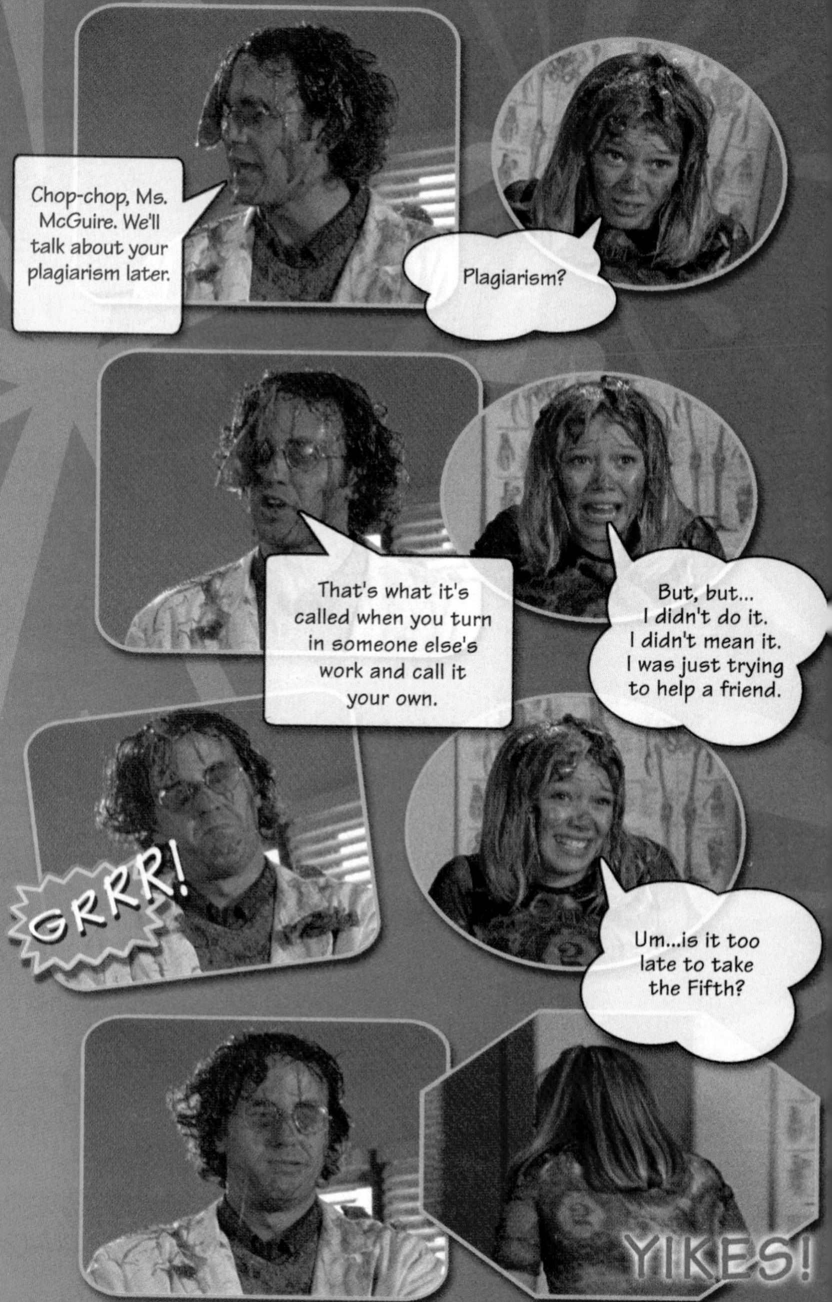
Chop-chop, Ms. McGuire. We'll talk about your plagiarism later.
Plagiarism?
That's what it's called when you turn in someone else's work and call it your own.
But, but... I didn't do it. I didn't mean it. I was just trying to help a friend.
GRRR!
Um...is it too late to take the Fifth?
YIKES!

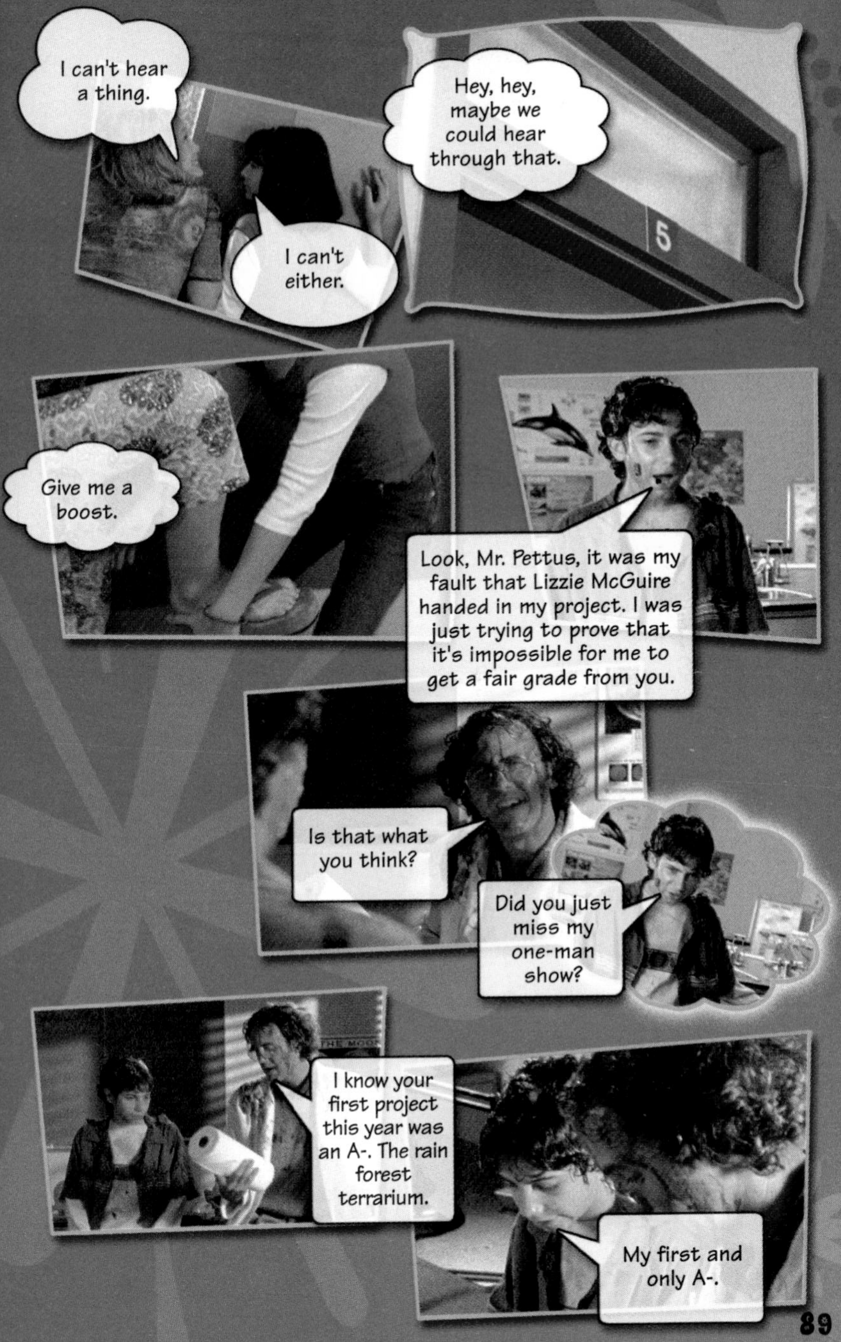
I can't hear a thing.
I can't either.
Hey, hey, maybe we could hear through that.
5
Give me a boost.
Look, Mr. Pettus, it was my fault that Lizzie McGuire handed in my project. I was just trying to prove that it's impossible for me to get a fair grade from you.
Is that what you think?
Did you just miss my one-man show?
I know your first project this year was an A-. The rain forest terrarium.
My first and only A-.

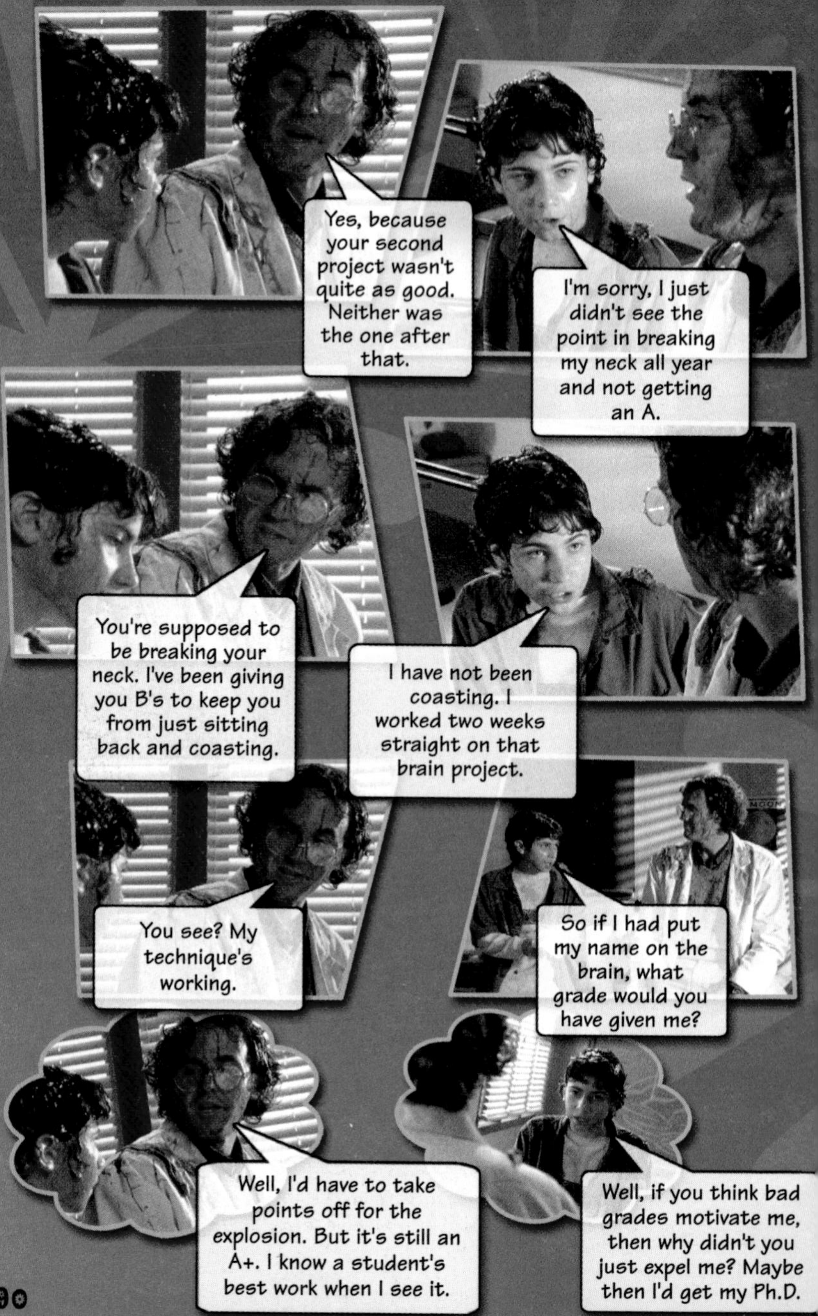
Yes, because your second project wasn't quite as good. Neither was the one after that.
I'm sorry, I just didn't see the point in breaking my neck all year and not getting an A.
You're supposed to be breaking your neck. I've been giving you B's to keep you from just sitting back and coasting.
I have not been coasting. I worked two weeks straight on that brain project.
You see? My technique's working.
So if I had put my name on the brain, what grade would you have given me?
Well, I'd have to take points off for the explosion. But it's still an A+. I know a student's best work when I see it.
Well, if you think bad grades motivate me, then why didn't you just expel me? Maybe then I'd get my Ph.D.

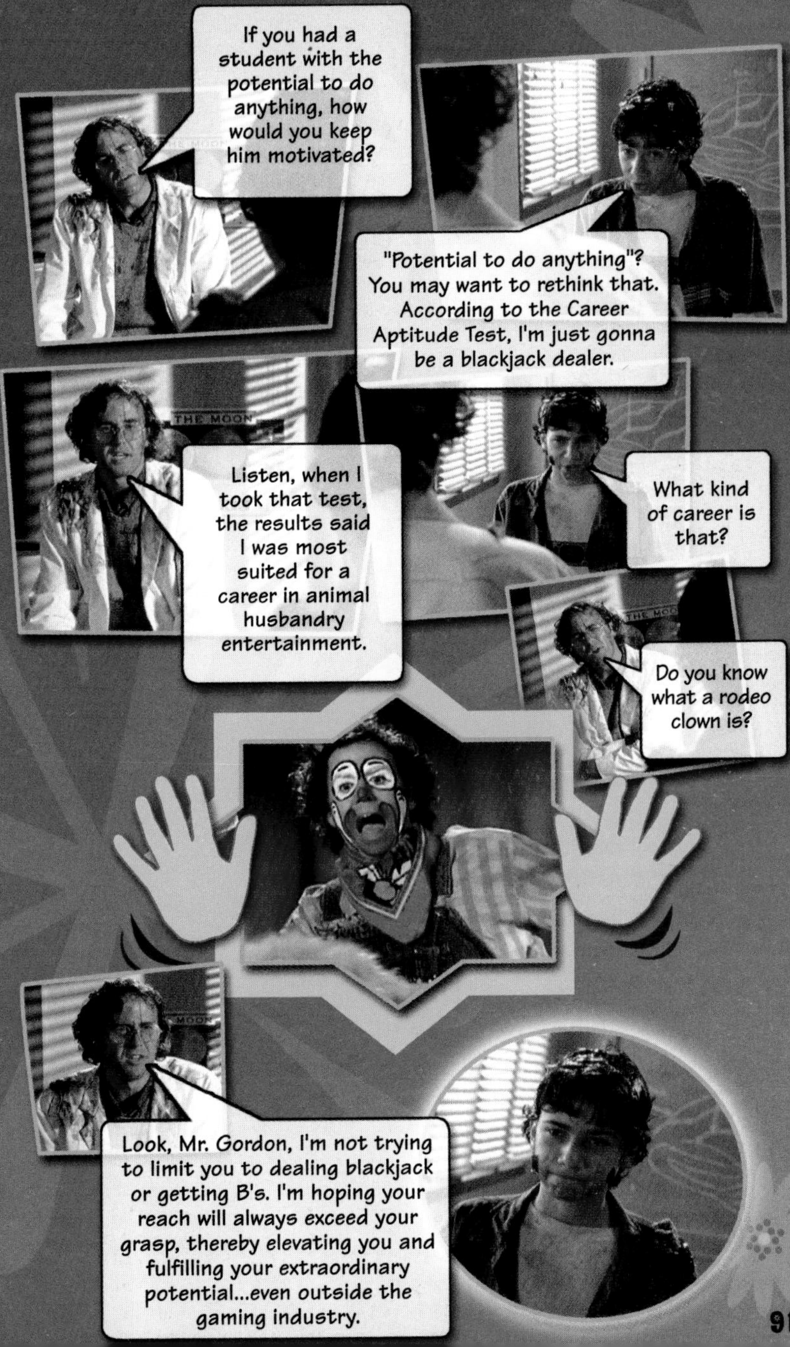
If you had a student with the potential to do anything, how would you keep him motivated?
"Potential to do anything"? You may want to rethink that. According to the Career Aptitude Test, I'm just gonna be a blackjack dealer.
Listen, when I took that test, the results said I was most suited for a career in animal husbandry entertainment.
What kind of career is that?
Do you know what a rodeo clown is?
Look, Mr. Gordon, I'm not trying to limit you to dealing blackjack or getting B's. I'm hoping your reach will always exceed your grasp, thereby elevating you and fulfilling your extraordinary potential...even outside the gaming industry.

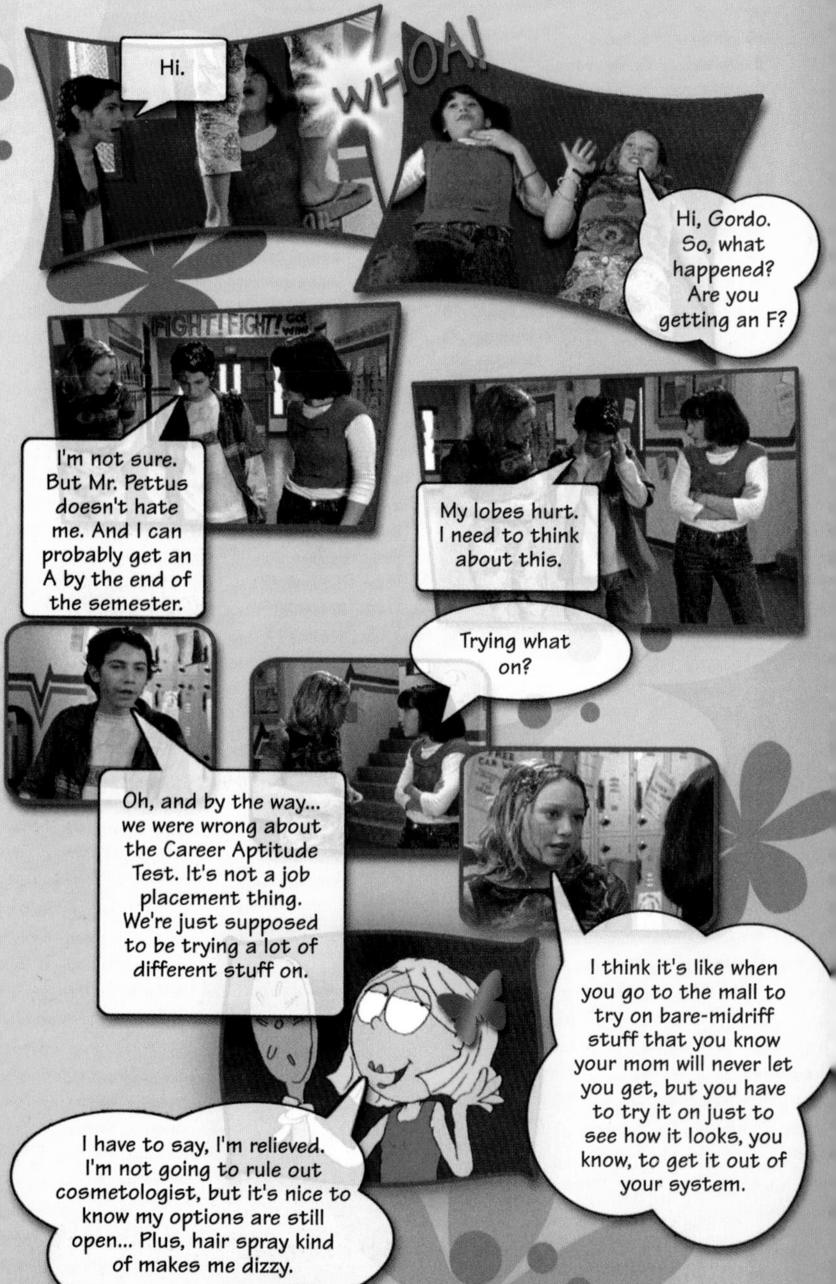

Hi.
WHOA!
Hi, Gordo. So, what happened? Are you getting an F?
I'm not sure. But Mr. Pettus doesn't hate me. And I can probably get an A by the end of the semester.
My lobes hurt. I need to think about this.
Oh, and by the way... we were wrong about the Career Aptitude Test. It's not a job placement thing. We're just supposed to be trying a lot of different stuff on.
Trying what on?
I think it's like when you go to the mall to try on bare-midriff stuff that you know your mom will never let you get, but you have to try it on just to see how it looks, you know, to get it out of your system.
I have to say, I'm relieved. I'm not going to rule out cosmetologist, but it's nice to know my options are still open... Plus, hair spray kind of makes me dizzy.

THAT NIGHT AT DINNER...

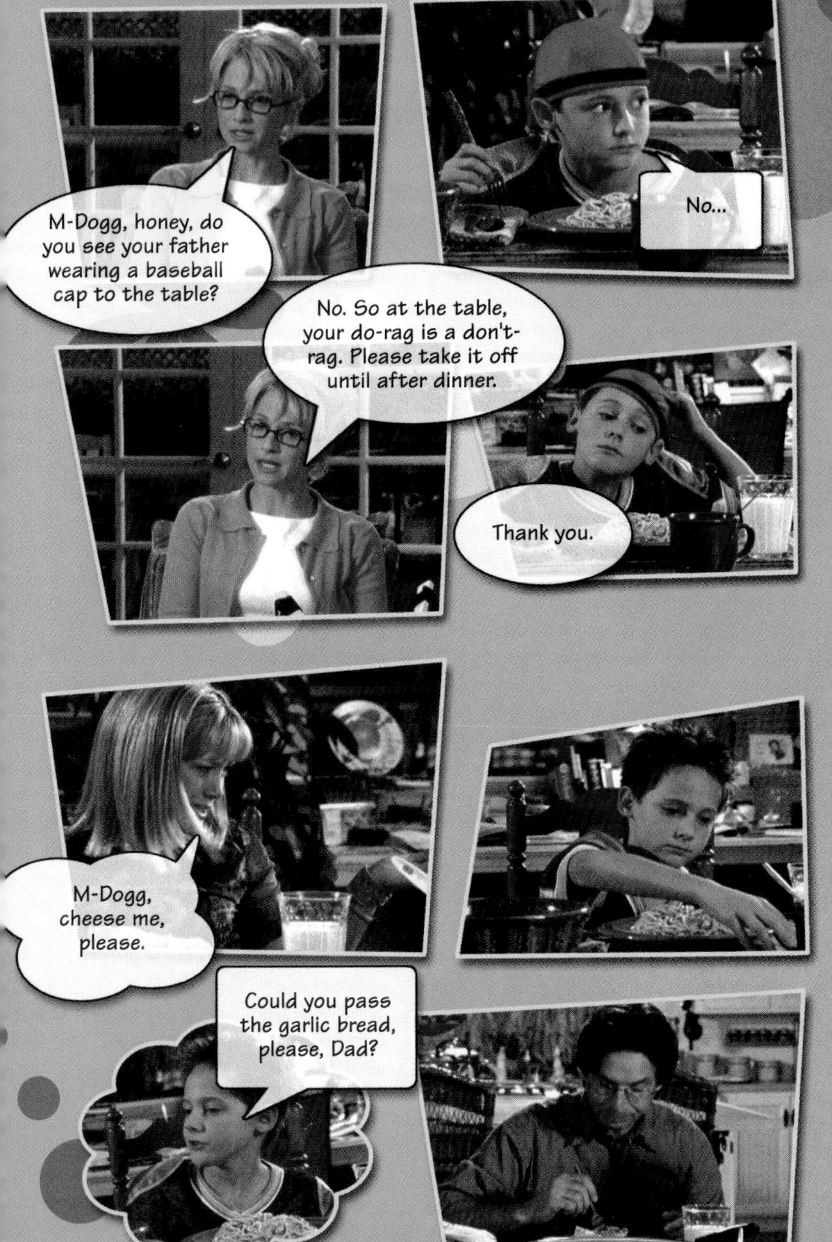
M-Dogg, honey, do you see your father wearing a baseball cap to the table?
No...
No. So at the table, your do-rag is a don't-rag. Please take it off until after dinner.
Thank you.
M-Dogg, cheese me, please.
Could you pass the garlic bread, please, Dad?

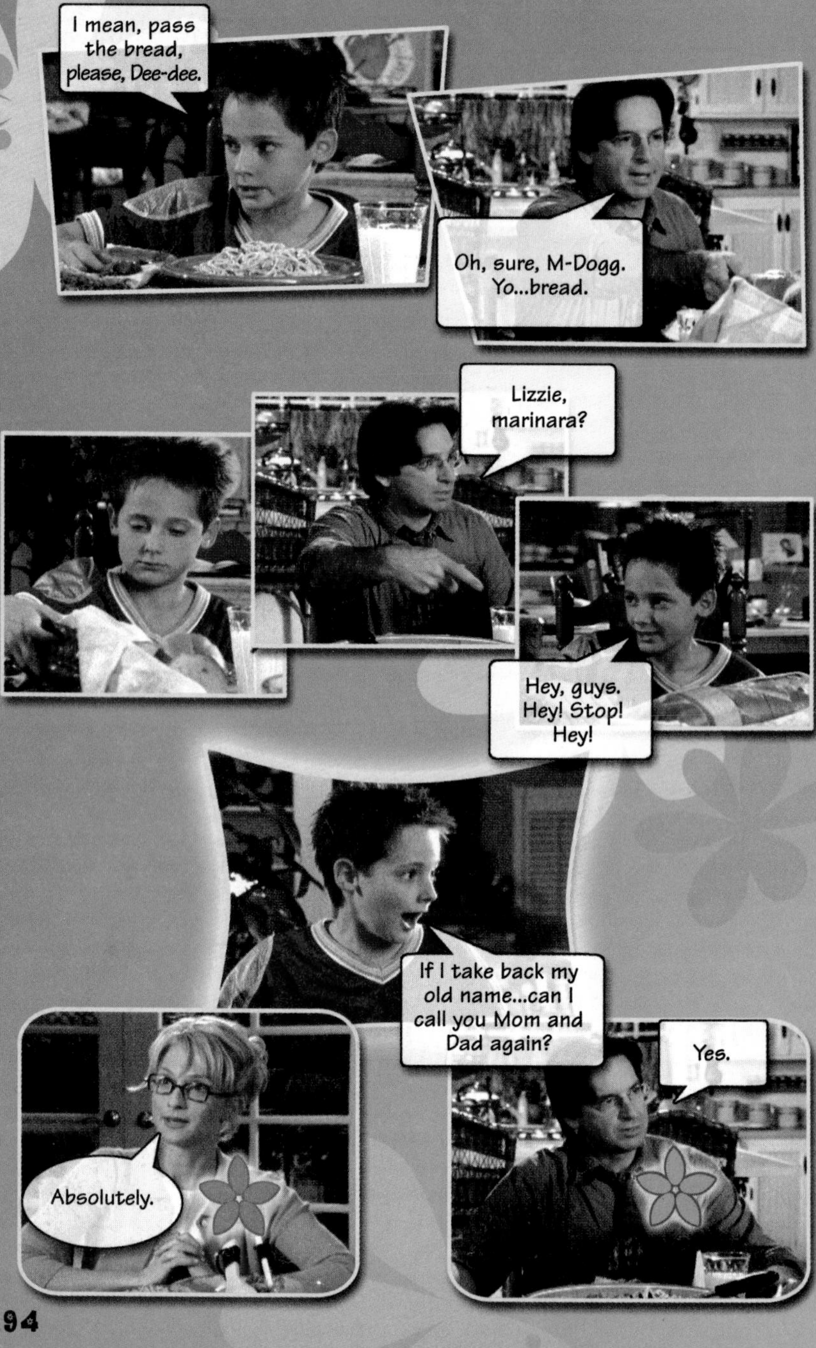
I mean, pass the bread, please, Dee-dee.
Oh, sure, M-Dogg. Yo...bread.
Lizzie, marinara?
Hey, guys. Hey! Stop! Hey!
If I take back my old name...can I call you Mom and Dad again?
Absolutely.
Yes.

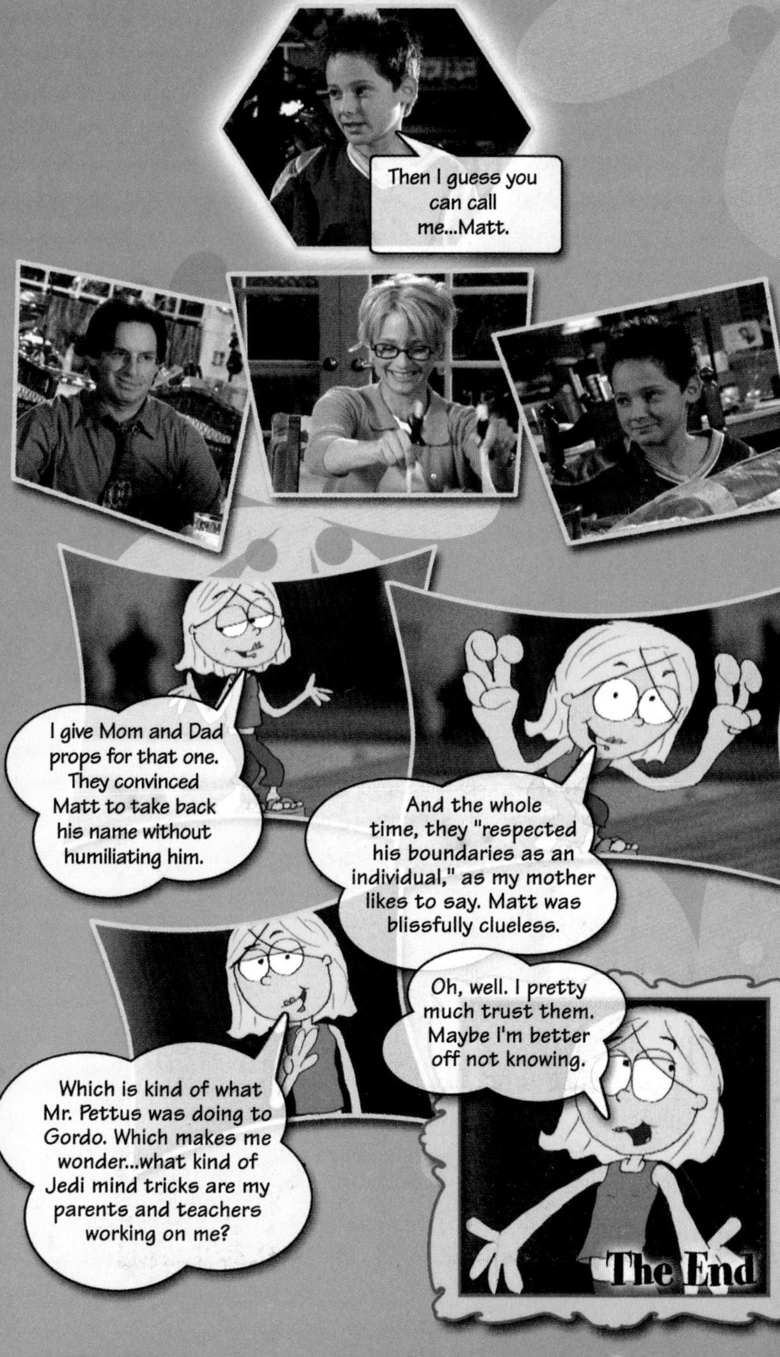
Then I guess you can call me...Matt.
I give Mom and Dad props for that one. They convinced Matt to take back his name without humiliating him.
And the whole time, they "respected his boundaries as an individual," as my mother likes to say. Matt was blissfully clueless.
Which is kind of what Mr. Pettus was doing to Gordo. Which makes me wonder...what kind of Jedi mind tricks are my parents and teachers working on me?
Oh, well. I pretty much trust them. Maybe I'm better off not knowing.
The End